Practice *Planners*®

Arthur E. Jongsma, Jr., Series Editor

Helping therapists help their clients...

TheraScribe®

The Treatment Planning and Clinical Record Management System for Mental Health Professionals.

TheraScribe®—the latest version of our popular treatment planning, patient record-keeping software. Facilitates intake/assessment reporting, progress monitoring, and outcomes analysis. Supports group treatment and multiprovider treatment teams. Compatible with our full array of **Practice*Planners*®** libraries, including our *Treatment Planner* software versions.

- This bestselling, easy-to-use Windows®-based software allows you to generate fully customized psychotherapy treatment plans that meet the requirements of all major accrediting agencies and most third-party payers.

- In just minutes, this user-friendly program's on-screen help enables you to create customized treatment plans.

- Praised in the *National Psychologist* and *Medical Software Reviews,* this innovative software simplifies and streamlines record-keeping.

- Available for a single user, or in a network version, this comprehensive software package suits the needs of all practices—both large and small.

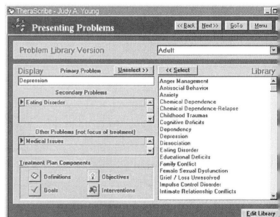

Treatment Planner Upgrade to Thera*Scribe*®

The behavioral definitions, goals, objectives, and interventions from this *Treatment Planner* can be imported into Thera*Scribe*®. For purchase and pricing information, please send in the coupon below or call 1-800-753-0655 or e-mail us at planners@wiley.com.

For more information about **Thera*Scribe*®** or the Upgrade to this *Treatment Planner,* fill in this coupon and mail it to: R. Crucitt, John Wiley & Sons, Inc., 7222 Commerce Center Dr., Ste. 240, Colorado Springs, CO 80919 or e-mail us at planners@wiley.com.

❏ Please send me information on **Thera*Scribe*®**

❏ Please send me information on the *Treatment Planner* Upgrade to **Thera*Scribe*®**
Name of *Treatment Planner*_____

❏ Please send me information on the network version of **Thera*Scribe*®**

Name_____

Affiliation_____

Address_____

City/State/Zip_____

Phone_____E-mail_____

For a free demo, visit us on the web at: www.wiley.com/therascribe

WILE

Practice*Planners*® Order Form

Treatment Planners cover all the necessary elements for developing formal treatment plans, including detailed problem definitions, long-term goals, short-term objectives, therapeutic interventions, and DSM-IV diagnoses.

Documentation Sourcebooks provide a comprehensive collection of ready-to-use blank forms, handouts, and questionnaires to help you manage your client reports and streamline the record keeping and treatment process. Features clear, concise explanations of the purpose of each form—including when it should be used and at what point. Includes customizable forms on disk.

e Complete Adult Psychotherapy Treatment Planner, Second Edition
0-471-31924-4 / $44.95

e Child Psychotherapy Treatment Planner, Second Edition
0-471-34764-7 / $44.95

e Adolescent Psychotherapy Treatment Planner, Second Edition
0-471-34766-3 / $44.95

e Chemical Dependence Treatment Planner
0-471-23795-7 / $44.95

e Continuum of Care Treatment Planner
0-471-19568-5 / $44.95

e Couples Psychotherapy Treatment Planner
0-471-24711-1 / $44.95

e Employee Assistance (EAP) Treatment Planner
0-471-24709-X / $44.95

e Pastoral Counseling Treatment Planner
0-471-25416-9 / $44.95

e Older Adult Psychotherapy Treatment Planner
0-471-29574-4 / $44.95

e Behavioral Medicine Treatment Planner
0-471-31923-6 / $44.95

e Group Therapy Treatment Planner
0-471-37449-0 / $44.95

e Family Therapy Treatment Planner
0-471-34768-X / $44.95

e Severe and Persistent Mental Illness Treatment Planner
0-471-35945-9 / $44.95

e Gay and Lesbian Psychotherapy Treatment Planner
0-471-35080-X / $44.95

The Clinical Documentation Sourcebook, Second Edition
0-471-32692-5 / $49.95

The Psychotherapy Documentation Primer
0-471-28990-6 / $45.00

The Couple and Family Clinical Documentation Sourcebook
0-471-25234-4 / $49.95

The Clinical Child Documentation Sourcebook
0-471-29111-0 / $49.95

The Chemical Dependence Treatment Documentation Sourcebook
0-471-31285-1 / $49.95

The Forensic Documentation Sourcebook
0-471-25459-2 / $85.00

The Continuum of Care Clinical Documentation Sourcebook
0-471-34581-4 / $75.00

NEW AND FORTHCOMING

The Traumatic Events Treatment Planner
0-471-39587-0 / $44.95

The Special Education Treatment Planner
0-471-38873-4 / $44.95

The Mental Retardation and Developmental Disability Treatment Planner
0-471-38253-1 / $44.95

The Social Work and Human Services Treatment Planner
0-471-37741-4 / $44.95

The Rehabilitation Psychology Treatment Planner
0-471-35178-4 / $44.95

Name_____

Affiliation_____

Address_____

City/State/Zip_____

Phone/Fax_____

E-mail_____

www.wiley.com/practiceplanners

To order, call 1-800-753-0655
(Please refer to promo #1-4019 when ordering.)
Or send this page with payment* to:
John Wiley & Sons, Inc., Attn: J. Knott
605 Third Avenue, New York, NY 10158-0012

❑ Check enclosed   ❑ Visa   ❑ MasterCard   ❑ American Express

Card #_____

Expiration Date_____

Signature_____

*Please add your local sales tax to all orders.

The Crisis Counseling
and Traumatic Events
Treatment Planner

PRACTICE *PLANNERS*™ SERIES

Treatment *Planners*

The Chemical Dependence Treatment Planner
The Continuum of Care Treatment Planner
The Couples Psychotherapy Treatment Planner
The Employee Assistance Treatment Planner
The Pastoral Counseling Treatment Planner
The Older Adult Psychotherapy Treatment Planner
The Complete Adult Psychotherapy Treatment Planner, 2e
The Behavioral Medicine Treatment Planner
The Group Therapy Treatment Planner
The Gay and Lesbian Psychotherapy Treatment Planner
The Child Psychotherapy Treatment Planner, 2e
The Adolescent Psychotherapy Treatment Planner, 2e
The Family Therapy Treatment Planner
The Severe and Persistent Mental Illness Treatment Planner
The Mental Retardation and Developmental Disability Treatment Planner
The Social Work and Human Services Treatment Planner
The Crisis Counseling and Traumatic Events Treatment Planner
The Rehabilitation Psychology Treatment Planner
The Personality Disorders Treatment Planner

Progress Notes *Planners*

The Adult Psychotherapy Progress Notes Planner
The Child Psychotherapy Progress Notes Planner
The Adolescent Psychotherapy Progress Notes Planner

Homework *Planners*

Brief Therapy Homework Planner
Brief Couples Therapy Homework Planner
Chemical Dependence Treatment Homework Planner
Brief Child Therapy Homework Planner
Brief Adolescent Therapy Homework Planner
Brief Employee Assistance Homework Planner
Brief Family Therapy Homework Planner

Documentation *Sourcebooks*

The Clinical Documentation Sourcebook
The Forensic Documentation Sourcebook
The Psychotherapy Documentation Primer
The Chemical Dependence Treatment Documentation Sourcebook
The Clinical Child Documentation Sourcebook
The Couple and Family Clinical Documentation Sourcebook
The Clinical Documentation Sourcebook, 2e
The Continuum of Care Clinical Documentation Sourcebook

PracticePlanners®

Arthur E. Jongsma, Jr., Series Editor

The Crisis Counseling and Traumatic Events Treatment Planner

Tammi D. Kolski

Michael Avriette

Arthur E. Jongsma, Jr.

JOHN WILEY & SONS, INC.

New York • Chichester • Weinheim • Brisbane • Singapore • Toronto

Published by John Wiley & Sons, Inc.
Published simultaneously in Canada.

All references to diagnostic codes and the entire content of Appendix B are reprinted with permission from the *Diagnostic and Statistical Manual of Mental Disorders, Fourth Edition.* Copyright 1994. American Psychiatric Association.

Library of Congress Cataloging-in-Publication Data:

Kolski, Tammi.
 The traumatic events treatment planner / Tammi Kolski, Michael Avriette, Arthur E. Jongsma, Jr.
  p. cm. — (Practice planners series)
  ISBN 0-471-39587-0 (paper : alk. paper) — ISBN 0-471-39588-9 (paper/disk : alk. paper)
  1. Life change events—Handbooks, manuals, etc. 2. Psychic trauma—Handbooks, manuals, etc. 3. Crisis intervention (Mental health services)—Handbooks, manuals, etc. 4. Stress (Psychology)—Handbooks, manuals, etc. 5. Mental health counseling—Handbooks, manuals, etc. I. Avriette, Michael. II. Jongsma, Arthur E., 1943– III. Title. IV. Practice planners.

 RC455.4.L53 .K65 2001
 616.85′21—dc21

                                                                                      00-043922

Printed in the United States of America.
10 9 8 7 6 5 4 3 2 1

CONTENTS

PRACTICE PLANNER SERIES PREFACE

The practice of psychotherapy has a dimension that did not exist 30, 20, or even 15 years ago—accountability. Treatment programs, public agencies, clinics, and even group and solo practitioners must now justify the treatment of patients to outside review entities that control the payment of fees. This development has resulted in an explosion of paperwork.

Clinicians must now document what has been done in treatment, what is planned for the future, and what the anticipated outcomes of the interventions are. The books and software in this Practice Planner series are designed to help practitioners fulfill these documentation requirements efficiently and professionally.

The Practice Planner series is growing rapidly. It now includes the second editions of the *Complete Adult Psychotherapy Treatment Planner,* the *Adolescent Psychotherapy Treatment Planner,* and the *Child Psychotherapy Treatment Planner.* Additional Treatment Planners are targeted to specialty areas of practice, including: chemical dependency, the continuum of care, couples therapy, employee assistance, behavioral medicine, therapy with older adults, pastoral counseling, family therapy, group therapy, neuropsychology, therapy with gays and lesbians, and more.

In addition to the Treatment Planners, the series also includes *TheraScribe®,* the latest version of the popular treatment planning, patient record-keeping software, as well as adjunctive books, such as the *Brief, Chemical Dependence, Couple, Child,* and *Adolescent Therapy Homework Planners, The Psychotherapy Documentation Primer,* and *Clinical, Forensic, Child, Couples and Family, Continuum of Care,* and *Chemical Dependence Documentation Sourcebooks*—containing forms and resources to aid in mental health practice management. Finally, the most recent additions to the Practical Planner series are the Psychotherapy Progress Notes Planners for adults, adolescents, and children, respectively. These books feature over 1,000 prewritten progress notes. Components are organized around presenting problems covered in the specific Treatment Planners written for adults, adolescents, and children. The goal of the series is to provide practitioners with the resources they need in order to provide high-quality care in the era of accountability—or, to put it simply, we seek to help you spend more time on patients, and less time on paperwork.

ARTHUR E. JONGSMA, JR.
Grand Rapids, Michigan

PREFACE

The Traumatic Events Treatment Planner was developed in response to the sad state of affairs in today's society. People have become exposed to violent crises at an incidence rate that is increasing alarmingly. Individuals in crisis need specialized interventions that are unlike other forms of therapy. This Treatment Planner provides a framework to offer crisis intervention effectively while incorporating the criteria necessary for managed care review and insurance reimbursement. While several books have been written to address individual traumatic events and effective means for successful recovery from such traumas, this Treatment Planner is the first of its kind in that it proposes a menu for treating many different traumas. While many clinicians specialize in specific treatment modalities or in treating limited patient populations, we must be prepared to assist any of our patients since traumatic events can and do occur to anyone. This Planner will assist the most skilled clinician, as well as the most inexperienced, in delivering effective crisis intervention.

Critical incident stress debriefing (CISD) is a fundamental tool of crisis intervention. Critical incident stress debriefing is not a new concept. Its development and implementation began in response to the needs of people affected by war. Though not new, CISD does require specialized training. The actual debriefing is a formal, seven-phase process of:

1. Establishing ground rules with particular emphasis upon confidentiality
2. Expression of the facts of the traumatic event as the individual experienced them
3. Identification and validation of the acute stress reactions experienced
4. Identification of any connection between the individual's personal life history and the trauma
5. Exploration of critical incident stress reactions not previously identified

6. Effective stress management education
7. Preparation to return to normal functioning

The International Critical Incident Stress Foundation, under the leadership of Dr. Jeffery Mitchell and Dr. George Everly, has researched and refined the CISD process and offers training internationally on the technique. The American Red Cross, the National Organization of Victim Assistance, and other organizations also provide information on how to conduct a CISD utilizing the framework as developed by Dr. Jeffery Mitchell. Though it is beyond the scope of this Treatment Planner to train a clinician in facilitating a CISD, there are several individuals and teams throughout the world who are trained in offering this intervention. These individuals/teams can, and should, be utilized as appropriate for an effective treatment intervention.

Our families have offered us much support and patience in the writing of this book. We thank them for that encouragement. This was Tammi's first experience in writing for this Treatment Planner series. The guidance of Michael and Art, the "experienced authors," made the completion of this book possible. To Russ and Ashleigh Kolski and to David and Aline Stebleton, thank you. Michael would like to thank Mitchell Willis at the American Red Cross for his support, information, and encouragement. Jen Byrne deserves our appreciation for her patient hours of word processing and assistance in compiling the final manuscript, in spite of our computer fumblings. Cristina Wojdylo, the new editor's assistant at John Wiley & Sons, has been a very welcome addition to the Practice Planner team. She has graciously and efficiently managed a myriad of details relating to the preparation of the manuscript for production. Thanks much, Cristina! Finally, we want to thank Peggy Alexander, our new editor at Wiley, who pushed for this book's completion and is the new energetic force behind the Practice Planner series.

Tammi D. Kolski
Michael Avriette
Arthur E. Jongsma, Jr.

INTRODUCTION

Since the early 1960s, formalized treatment planning has gradually become a vital aspect of the entire health care delivery system, whether it is treatment related to physical health, mental health, child welfare, or substance abuse. What started in the medical sector in the 1960s spread into the mental health sector in the 1970s as clinics, psychiatric hospitals, agencies, and so on, began to seek accreditation from bodies such as the Joint Commission on Accreditation of Healthcare Organizations (JCAHO) to qualify for third-party reimbursements. For most treatment providers to achieve accreditation, they had to begin developing and strengthening their documentation skills in the area of treatment planning. Previously, most mental health and substance abuse treatment providers had, at best, a "bare-bones" plan that looked similar for most of the individuals they treated. Treatment planning for crisis intervention work was basically unheard of. As a result, clients were uncertain as to what they were trying to attain in mental health treatment. Goals were vague, objectives were nonexistent, and interventions were applied equally to all clients regardless of the duration of treatment. Outcome data were not measurable, and neither the treatment provider nor the client knew exactly when treatment changed from crisis intervention to ongoing outpatient therapy and when treatment was complete. The initial development of rudimentary treatment plans for crisis intervention and beyond made inroads toward addressing some of these issues.

With the advent of managed care in the 1980s, treatment planning has taken on even more importance. Managed care systems recognize crisis intervention as an integral part of an individual's recovery from trauma. Yet managed care systems *insist* that clinicians rapidly develop a crisis intervention treatment plan. The goal of most managed care companies is to expedite the treatment process by prompting the client and treatment provider to focus on identifying and changing behavioral problems as quickly as possible. Treatment plans must be specific as to the problems and interventions, individualized to meet the client's needs and goals, and measurable in terms of setting milestones that can be used to chart the patient's progress. Pressure from third-party payers, accrediting agencies, and other outside parties has therefore increased the need for clinicians to produce effective, high-quality treatment plans in a short time frame. However, many mental health providers have little experience in treatment plan development. Our purpose in writing this book is to clarify, simplify, and accelerate the treatment planning process, starting with crisis intervention.

TREATMENT PLAN UTILITY

Detailed written treatment plans can benefit not only the client, therapist, treatment team, insurance community, and treatment agency, but also the overall psychotherapy profession. The client is served by a written plan because it stipulates the issues that are the focus of the treatment process. It is very easy for both provider and client to lose sight of what the traumatic issues were that brought the patient into therapy as outpatient counseling services continue. The treatment plan is a guide that structures the focus of the therapeutic contract. Since issues can change as therapy progresses, the treatment plan must be viewed as a dynamic document that can and must be updated to reflect any major change of problem, definition, goal, objective, or intervention. Clients and therapists benefit from the treatment plan, which forces both to think about therapy outcomes. Behaviorally stated, measurable objectives clearly focus the treatment endeavor. Clients no longer have to wonder what therapy is trying to accomplish from the crisis intervention forward. Clear objectives also allow the patient to channel effort into specific changes that will lead to the long-term goal of problem resolution. Crisis intervention is no longer a vague contract to just talk honestly and openly about emotions and cognitions until the client feels better. Both client and therapist are concentrating on specifically stated objectives using specific interventions.

Providers are aided by treatment plans because they are forced to think analytically and critically about therapeutic interventions that are best suited for objective attainment for the patient. Therapists were traditionally trained to "follow the patient," but now a formalized plan is the guide to the treatment process. The therapist must give advance attention to the technique, approach, assignment, or cathartic target that will form the basis for interventions.

Clinicians benefit from clear documentation of treatment because it provides a measure of added protection from possible patient litigation. Malpractice suits are increasing in frequency and insurance premiums are soaring. The first line of defense against allegations is a complete clinical record detailing the treatment process. A written, individualized, formal treatment plan that is the guideline for the crisis evaluation and following therapeutic process, that has been reviewed and signed by the client, and that is coupled with problem-oriented progress notes is a powerful defense against exaggerated or false claims.

A well-crafted treatment plan that clearly stipulates presenting problems and intervention strategies facilitates the crisis intervention and following treatment process carried out by team members in inpatient, residential, or intensive outpatient settings. Good communication between team members about what approach is being implemented and who is responsible for which intervention is critical. Team meetings which were held to discuss patients in crisis used to be the only source of interaction between providers; often, therapeutic conclusions or assignments were not recorded. Now, a thorough treatment plan stipulates in writing the details of objectives and the varied interventions (pharmacologic, milieu, group therapy, didactic, recreational, individual therapy, etc.) and who will implement them.

Every treatment agency or institution is constantly looking for ways to increase the quality and uniformity of the documentation in the clinical record. A standardized, written treatment plan with problem definitions, goals, objectives, and interventions in every client's file enhances that uniformity of documentation. This uniformity eases the task of record reviewers inside and outside the agency. Outside reviewers, such as JCAHO, insist on documentation that clearly outlines a crisis intervention treatment plan, progress, and discharge status.

The demand for accountability from third-party payers and health maintenance organizations (HMOs) is partially satisfied by a written treatment plan and complete progress notes. More and more managed care systems are demanding a structured therapeutic contract that has measurable objectives and explicit interventions, even for crisis intervention. Clinicians cannot avoid this move toward being accountable to those outside the treatment process.

The psychotherapy profession stands to benefit from the use of more precise, measurable objectives to evaluate success in crisis intervention and ongoing mental health treatment. With the advent of detailed treatment plans, outcome data can be more easily collected for interventions that are effective in achieving specific goals.

HOW TO DEVELOP A TREATMENT PLAN

The process of developing a treatment plan involves a logical series of steps that build on each other much like constructing a house. The foundation of any effective treatment plan is the data gathered in a thorough biopsychosocial assessment. As the client has survived a traumatic event, the clinician must sensitively listen to and understand what the client struggles with in terms of emotional status, social network, physical health, coping skills, interpersonal conflicts, self-esteem, family of origin issues, and so on. Assessment data may be gathered from a social history, physical exam, clinical interview, psychological testing, or contact with a client's significant others. The integration of the data by the clinician or the multidisciplinary treatment team members is critical for understanding the client, as is an awareness of the basis of the client's struggle. We have identified six specific steps for developing an effective treatment plan based on the assessment data.

Step One: Problem Selection

Although the client is presenting as a result of surviving an identified crisis, the clinician must determine if there are other issues complicating the client's presentation. Usually, the *primary* problem will be the recent trauma the client experienced, and *secondary* problems are issues that were likely present prior to the crisis occurring. Some *other* problems may have to be set aside as not urgent enough to require treatment at this time. An effective treatment plan can only deal with a few selected problems or treatment will lose its direction. This Planner offers 26 crisis situations or expected problems as a result of the trauma from which to select those that most accurately represent your client's presenting issues.

As the client progresses from crisis intervention to an ongoing outpatient therapy relationship, it is important to include opinions from the client as to his or her prioritization of issues for which help is being sought. A client's motivation to participate in and cooperate with the treatment process depends, to some extent, on the degree to which treatment addresses his or her greatest needs.

Step Two: Problem Definition

Each individual client presents with unique nuances as to how crisis reactions are revealed in his or her life. Therefore, each problem that is selected for treatment focus requires a specific definition about how it is evidenced in the particular client. The symptom pattern should be associated with diagnostic criteria and codes such as those found in the *Diagnostic and Statistical Manual* or the *International Classification of Diseases*. The Planner, following the pattern established by *DSM-IV*, offers such behaviorally specific definition statements to choose from or to serve as a model for your own personally crafted statements. You will find several behavior symptoms or syndromes listed that may characterize one of the 26 presenting problems.

Step Three: Goal Development

The next step in treatment plan development is that of setting broad goals for the resolution of the target problem. These statements need not be crafted in measurable terms but can be global, long-term goals that indicate a desired positive outcome to the treatment procedures. The Planner suggests several possible goal statements for each problem, but one statement is all that is required in a treatment plan.

Step Four: Objective Construction

In contrast to long-term goals, objectives must be stated in behaviorally measurable language. It must be clear when the client has achieved the established objectives; therefore, vague, subjective objectives are not acceptable. Review agencies (e.g., JCAHO), HMOs, and managed care organizations insist that psychological treatment outcomes be measurable. The objectives presented in this Planner are designed to meet this demand for accountability. Numerous alternatives are presented to allow construction of a variety of treatment plan possibilities for the same presenting problem. The clinician must exercise professional judgment as to which objectives are most appropriate for a given client.

Each objective should be developed as a step toward attaining the broad treatment goal. In essence, objectives can be thought of as a series of steps that, when completed, will result in the achievement of the long-term goal. There should be at least two objectives for each problem, but the clinician may construct as many as are necessary for goal achievement. Target attainment dates should be listed for each objective. New objectives should be added to the plan as the individual's treatment progresses. When all the necessary objectives have been achieved, the client should have resolved the target problem successfully.

Step Five: Intervention Creation

Interventions are the actions of the clinician designed to help the client complete the objectives. There should be at least one intervention for every objective. If the client does not accomplish the objective after the initial intervention, new interventions should be added to the plan. Interventions should be selected on the basis of the client's needs and the treatment provider's full therapeutic repertoire. This Planner contains interventions from a broad range of therapeutic approaches, including cognitive, dynamic, behavioral, pharmacologic, family-oriented, and solution-focused brief therapy. Other interventions may be written by the provider to reflect his or her own training and experience. The addition of new problems, definitions, goals, objectives, and interventions to those found in the Planner is encouraged because doing so adds to the database for future reference and use.

Some suggested interventions listed in the Planner refer to specific books that can be assigned to the client for adjunctive bibliotherapy. Appendix A contains a full bibliographic reference list of these materials. The books are arranged under each problem for which they are appropriate as assigned reading for clients. When a book is used as part of an intervention plan, it should be reviewed with the client after it is read, enhancing the application of the content of the book to the specific client's circumstances. For further information about self-help books, mental health professionals may wish to consult *The Authoritative Guide to Self-Help Books* (1994) by Santrock, Minnett, and Campbell (available from The Guilford Press, New York, NY).

Assigning an intervention to a specific provider is most relevant if the patient is being treated by a team in an inpatient, residential, or intensive outpatient setting. Within these settings, personnel other than the primary clinician may be responsible for implementing a specific intervention. Review agencies require that the responsible provider's name be stipulated for every intervention.

Step Six: Diagnosis Determination

The determination of an appropriate diagnosis is based on an evaluation of the client's complete clinical presentation. The clinician must compare the behavioral, cognitive, emotional, and interpersonal symptoms that the client presents to the criteria for diagnosis of a mental illness condition as described in *DSM-IV*. The issue of differential diagnosis is admittedly a difficult one that research has shown to have rather low interrater reliability. Psychologists have also been trained to think more in terms of maladaptive behavior than disease labels. In spite of these factors, diagnosis is a reality that exists in the world of mental health care, and it is a necessity for third-party reimbursement. (However, recently, managed care agencies are more interested in behavioral indices that are exhibited by the client than the actual diagnosis.) It is the clinician's thorough knowledge of *DSM-IV* criteria and a complete understanding of the client assessment data that contribute to the most reliable, valid diagnosis. An accurate assessment of behavioral indicators will also contribute to more effective treatment planning.

HOW TO USE THIS PLANNER

Our experience has taught us that learning the skills of effective treatment plan writing can be a tedious and difficult process for many clinicians. It is more stressful to try to develop this expertise when under the pressure of increased patient load and short time frames placed on clinicians today by managed care systems. The documentation demands can be overwhelming when we must move quickly from evaluation to crisis intervention treatment plan to progress notes. In the process, we must be very specific about how and when objectives can be achieved, and how progress is exhibited in each client. *The Traumatic Events Treatment Planner* was developed as a tool to aid clinicians in writing a treatment plan in a rapid manner that is clear, specific, and highly individualized according to the following progression:

1. Choose one presenting problem (Step One), usually being the traumatic event the client experienced. Locate the corresponding page number for that problem in the Planner's table of contents.
2. Select two or three of the listed behavioral definitions (Step Two) and record them in the appropriate section on your treatment plan form. Feel free to add your own defining statement if you determine that your client's behavioral manifestation of the identified problem is not listed. (Note that while our design for treatment planning is vertical, it will work equally well on plan forms formatted horizontally.)
3. Select a single long-term goal (Step Three) and again write the selection, exactly as it is written in the Planner or in some appropriately modified form, in the corresponding area of your own form.
4. Review the listed objectives for this problem and select the ones that you judge to be clinically indicated for your client (Step Four). Remember, it is recommended that you select at least two objectives for each problem. Add a target date or the number of sessions allocated for the attainment of each objective.
5. Choose relevant interventions (Step Five). The Planner offers suggested interventions related to each objective in the parentheses following the objective statement. But do not limit yourself to those interventions. The entire list is eclectic and may

offer options that are more tailored to your theoretical approach or preferred way of working with clients. Also, just as with definitions, goals, and objectives, there is space allowed for you to enter your own interventions into the Planner. This allows you to refer to these entries when you create a plan around this problem in the future. You will have to assign responsibility to a specific person for implementation of each intervention if the treatment is being carried out by a multidisciplinary team.

6. Several *DSM-IV* diagnoses are listed at the end of each chapter that are commonly associated with a client who has this problem. These diagnoses are meant to be suggestions for clinical consideration. Select a diagnosis listed or assign a more appropriate choice from the *DSM-IV* (Step Six).

    Note: To accommodate those practitioners that tend to plan treatment in terms of diagnostic labels rather than presenting problems, Appendix B lists all of the *DSM-IV* diagnoses that have been presented in the various presenting problem chapters as suggestions for consideration. Each diagnosis is followed by the presenting problem that has been associated with that diagnosis. The provider may look up the presenting problems for a selected diagnosis to review definitions, goals, objectives, and interventions that may be appropriate for their clients with that diagnosis.

Congratulations! You should now have a complete, individualized treatment plan that is ready for immediate implementation and presentation to the client. It should resemble the format of the sample plan presented on page 10.

A FINAL NOTE

One important aspect of effective treatment planning is that each plan should be tailored to the individual client's problems and needs. Treatment plans should not be mass produced, even if clients have similar problems. The individual's strengths and weaknesses, unique stressors, social network, family circumstances, and symptom patterns *must* be considered in developing a treatment strategy. Drawing upon our own years of clinical experience, we have put together a variety of treatment choices. These statements can be combined in thousands of permutations to develop detailed treatment plans. Relying on their own good judgment, clinicians can easily select the statements that are appropriate for the individuals they are treating. In addition, we encourage readers to add their own definitions, goals, objectives, and interventions to the existing samples. It is our hope that *The Traumatic Events Treatment Planner* will promote effective, creative treatment planning starting with crisis intervention—a process that will ultimately benefit the client, clinician, and mental health community.

SAMPLE TREATMENT PLAN

PROBLEM: DISASTER

Definitions: Involvement in a natural disaster (e.g., tornado, flood, hurricane, blizzard, volcano eruption, drought, earthquake, etc.).

Devastation of or extreme disruption to home, community, personal belongings, and/or daily operations.

Experiencing a fight-or-flight response of increased adrenaline, sensory acuity, increased heart rate, and/or hyperventilation.

Emotional reactions of shock, disbelief, confusion, helplessness, loss of control, irritability, survivor's guilt, anxiety, despair, fear, and/or grief.

Goal: Stabilize physical, cognitive, behavioral, and emotional reactions while increasing the ability to function on a daily basis.

Objectives

1. Establish shelter and consistently attend to basic needs of food, clothing, hygiene, and sleep. (9/20/00)

2. Describe what actions were performed before and during the disaster. (9/20/00)

Interventions

1. Assist the client and his/her family in locating a disaster shelter established by the American Red Cross or another disaster relief organization.

2. Respect the client's need for privacy and private grieving. Offer to make sleeping and identified space in the shelter as personal and comfortable as possible.

3. Encourage the client to eat well-balanced, hot meals as offered through community resources such as the American Red Cross.

1. Sensitively explore the client's recollection of facts about the disaster.

	2. Gently ask the client to recall his/her actions taken before, during, and immediately following the disaster, being careful not to press him/her into being overwhelmed.
3. Identify the sights, sounds, and physical discomforts endured during the disaster. (10/15/00)	1. Inquire as to what the client saw, heard, or physically felt when the disaster struck, being careful not to press him/her into being overwhelmed.
4. Verbalize an understanding of the cycle of recovery. (10/30/00)	1. Teach the client about the cycle of recovery when surviving a disaster (e.g., heroic phase, honeymoon phase, disillusionment phase, reconstruction phase).
	2. Express the appropriateness of grieving material losses (possessions) as well as the loss of future hopes and plans.

Diagnosis: 308.3   Acute Stress Disorder

Note: The numbers in parentheses accompanying the short-term objectives in each chapter correspond to the list of suggested therapeutic interventions in that chapter. Each objective has specific interventions that have been designed to assist the client in attaining that objective. Clinical judgment should determine the exact intervention to be used, including any outside of those suggested.

ACUTE STRESS DISORDER

BEHAVIORAL DEFINITIONS

1. Exposure to actual death of another or threatened death or serious injury to self or another, which resulted in an intense emotional response of fear, helplessness, or horror.
2. Experiences dissociative symptoms of numbing, detachment, derealization, depersonalization, amnesia, or reduction of awareness to surroundings.
3. Reexperience the event in thoughts, dreams, illusions, flashbacks, or recurrent images.
4. Marked avoidance of stimuli that arouse recollections of the trauma—whether through thoughts, feelings, conversations, activities, places, or people.
5. Symptoms of increased arousal such as difficulty sleeping, irritability, poor concentration, hypervigilance, exaggerated startle response, or motor restlessness.
6. Physical symptoms of chest pain, chest pressure, sweats, shortness of breath, headaches, muscle tension, intestinal upset, heart palpitations, or dry mouth.

__. _____
   _____
__. _____
   _____
__. _____
   _____

LONG-TERM GOALS

1. Stabilize physical, cognitive, behavioral, and emotional reactions to the trauma while increasing the ability to function on a daily basis.
2. Diminish intrusive images and the alteration in functioning or activity level that is due to stimuli associated with the trauma.
3. Assimilate the traumatic event into life experience without ongoing distress.
4. Confront, forgive, or accept the perpetrator of the traumatic event.

—. _____
_____
—. _____
_____
—. _____
_____

SHORT-TERM OBJECTIVES

1. Describe any bodily injury or physical symptom that has resulted from the trauma. (1, 2)
2. Describe the traumatic event, providing as much detail as comfort allows. (3, 4)
3. Describe the feelings that were experienced at the time of the trauma. (5)
4. Identify the impact that the traumatic event has had on daily functioning. (6, 7)
5. Avoid the geographic area surrounding the traumatic event. (8)
6. Identify distorted cognitive messages that promote fear

THERAPEUTIC INTERVENTIONS

1. Assist in getting the client to an urgent care or emergency department for medical consultation.
2. Make a referral to a physician for a medical evaluation.
3. Actively build a level of trust with the client in individual sessions through consistent eye contact, unconditional positive regard, and warm acceptance to help increase his/her ability to identify and express feelings.
4. Gently and sensitively explore the recollection of the facts of the traumatic incident.

and replace those messages with reality-based self-talk that nurtures confidence and calm. (9, 10)

7. Implement behavioral coping strategies that reduce tension. (11, 12)

8. Design an activity to be implemented on the anniversary day of the event or around major life events (i.e., holidays, graduation). (13, 14, 15)

9. Implement the stress inoculation activity and discuss the reaction after the trigger event has occurred. (15, 16)

10. Report the termination of flashback experiences. (17, 18)

11. Verbalize an increased understanding of the beliefs and images that produce fear, worry, or anxiety. (9, 19)

12. Cooperate with an evaluation for psychotropic medication. (20)

13. Take psychotropic medications as prescribed and report any side effects to appropriate professionals. (20, 21)

14. Decrease symptoms of autonomic arousal by learning and implementing relaxation techniques. (10, 22, 23, 24)

15. Increase daily social and vocational activities. (11, 25)

5. Explore the client's emotional reaction at the time of the trauma.

6. Ask the client to identify how the traumatic event has negatively impacted his/her life.

7. Administer psychological testing to assess the nature and severity of the emotional, cognitive, and behavioral impact of the trauma.

8. Encourage the client to develop alternative routes that don't involve exposure to the place of the traumatic event so as to avoid overwhelming stress reactions associated with exposure to the scene of the trauma.

9. Explore distorted cognitive messages that mediate negative emotional reactions to the trauma.

10. Help the client develop reality-based cognitive messages that will increase self-confidence and facilitate a reduction in fight-or-flight response.

11. Assist the client in developing behavioral coping strategies (i.e., increased social involvement, journaling, physical exercise) that will ameliorate the stress reactions.

12. Develop with the client a symptom onset timeline connected to the trauma.

13. Teach the client about the possible increase in emo-

16. Recall the details of the traumatic event accurately and without cognitive distortions or emotional devastation. (9, 26, 27, 28)

17. Place responsibility for the trauma on the perpetrator without equivocation. (29, 30)

18. Verbalize an understanding of the benefits and the process of forgiveness of the perpetrator. (31, 32)

19. Make a commitment to begin the process of forgiveness of the perpetrator. (33, 34, 35)

20. Attend a survivors' support group. (36)

___. _____
    _____

___. _____
    _____

___. _____
    _____

tional disturbance that is associated with the anniversary date or other significant days that trigger memories of the event.

14. Prompt the client to talk about how the pain, sense of loss, or alteration of life that has resulted from the traumatic event has increased with the approaching anniversary of the event or other trigger events (e.g., holidays, vacation, graduation, etc.).

15. Assist the client in preparing for trigger events or dates by planning involvement with people who have been supportive.

16. Ask the client to express the emotions experienced on the day of the trigger event (e.g., anniversary day, holiday, etc.).

17. Explore whether the client has had any flashback experiences to this trauma or previous traumatic events.

18. Prompt the client to describe the traumatic experience within the session noting whether he/she is overwhelmed with emotions; monitor for decrease in intensity and frequency of flashback experiences as therapy progresses from week to week.

19. Have the client write in a journal the recurring images or memories that are associated with the trauma.

20. Refer the client to a physician for a psychotropic medication evaluation.

21. Monitor the client's medication compliance and effectiveness. Confer with the physician regularly.

22. Train the client in guided imagery techniques that induce relaxation.

23. Train the client in the progressive muscle relaxation procedure.

24. Utilize biofeedback techniques to facilitate the client learning relaxation skills.

25. Encourage the client to return to work and/or a normal daily routine; phase into these activities gradually but steadily if necessary.

26. Ask the client to carefully recall all the details of the traumatic event verbally and/or in writing.

27. Consult with law enforcement, relatives, or coworkers who have facts and/or details regarding the event, to corroborate and/or elaborate on the client's recall.

28. Go with the client to the scene of the event while offering desensitization techniques to reduce stress reactions as they develop.

29. Assign the client to write a letter to the perpetrator of the trauma, expressing the anger, anxiety, and/or de-

pression that has resulted from the trauma.

30. Encourage and reinforce the client in placing clear responsibility for the traumatic event on the perpetrator(s) without taking on irrational, undue guilt for himself/herself.

31. Recommend that the client read *The Art of Forgiveness* (Smedes) to gain a healthier perspective on the benefits of forgiveness.

32. Teach the healing benefits and the process of forgiving anyone who has caused us severe pain.

33. Role-play with the client how an interaction with the perpetrator may take place, reinforcing the client's need for expression of pain as well as movement toward forgiveness.

34. Offer to meet with the client in a confrontation of the perpetrator of the trauma for the purpose of expressing pain, placing responsibility, and beginning the process of forgiveness.

35. Assign the client to write a letter to the perpetrator of the trauma for the purpose of expressing pain, placing responsibility, and beginning the process of forgiveness; process the letter in a session.

36. Refer the client to a survivors' support group that is

focused on the nature of the trauma to which the client was exposed.

__. _____
    _____

__. _____
    _____

__. _____
    _____

DIAGNOSTIC SUGGESTIONS

Axis I: 308.3   Acute Stress Disorder
              309.24   Adjustment Disorder with Anxiety
              309.28   Adjustment Disorder with Mixed Anxiety and
                         Depressed Mood
              300.02   Generalized Anxiety Disorder
              300.21   Panic Disorder with Agoraphobia
              300.01   Panic Disorder without Agoraphobia
              309.81   Posttraumatic Stress Disorder
              _____   _____

              _____   _____
Axis II: 301.6   Dependent Personality Disorder
              301.50   Histrionic Personality Disorder

              _____   _____

              _____   _____

CHILD ABUSE / NEGLECT

BEHAVIORAL DEFINITIONS

1. Wounds and/or bruises in different stages of healing that provide evidence of ongoing physical abuse.
2. Blood in underwear/genital region, sexually transmitted diseases, or tears in the vagina or anus that provide evidence of sexual abuse.
3. Report by self, parents, law enforcement, medical professionals, educators, and/or child protective services of intentional harm or a threat of harm by someone acting in the role of caretaker.
4. Caretaker fails to provide basic shelter, food, supervision, medical care, or support.
5. Coercive, demeaning, or overly distant behavior by a parent or other caretaker that interferes with normal social or psychological development.
6. Medical documentation of failure to thrive (weight below the 5th percentile for age) in infants or brain trauma secondary to violent shaking.
7. Inappropriate exposure to sexual acts or material, age-inappropriate knowledge and/or interest in sexual behavior (e.g., reaching for other's genitalia, masturbation of peers, discussing sexual activities, use of sexually oriented language, etc.).
8. Behaviors that are incongruent with chronological age such as thumb sucking, bed-wetting, clinging to the parent, and so on.
9. Repetitive play that reenacts situations regarding the abuse.
10. Nightmares, difficulty falling asleep.
11. Recurrent and intrusive recollections of the abuse.
12. Avoidance of situations related to the abuse, demonstrating fear when around the suspected abuser.
13. Explosive reactions of rage, anger, and/or aggression when exposed to the abuser or situations that trigger memories of the abuse.

14. Pronounced change in mood and affect such as depression, anxiety, and irritability.
15. Withdrawal from activities with peers, family, and school that were previously a source of pleasure.

—. _____
_____
_____

—. _____
_____
_____

—. _____
_____

LONG-TERM GOALS

1. Establish and maintain safety of the child.
2. Eliminate all abuse.
3. Develop appropriate boundaries within the family.
4. Return to previous level of psychosocial functioning as evidenced by an elimination of mood disturbance, a return to previously enjoyed activities, and the ability to recall the abusive incident(s) without regression.
5. Prevent the cycle of abuse from occurring with peers, spouses, the client's own children, and others.

—. _____
_____

—. _____
_____

—. _____
_____

SHORT-TERM OBJECTIVES

1. Identify the nature, frequency, and intensity of the abuse. (1, 2, 3, 4, 18)
2. Verbalize an understanding of the need for a report of

THERAPEUTIC INTERVENTIONS

1. Establish rapport with the child by providing reassurance, compassion, and trust. Use age-appropriate terminology and interact on

suspected abuse to be given to child protective services or other law enforcement authorities. (5, 6, 10)

3. Describe genitalia, what sex education/information has been obtained (and how recently), and what exposure to sexual practices he/she has had. (3, 7)

4. Move to a safe environment. (8, 9, 10)

5. Responsible adult authorizes and cooperates with the psychological and medical treatment of the child. (11)

6. Receive necessary medical care to treat any injuries. (12, 13)

7. School personnel collaborates with therapy goals and interventions. (14, 15)

8. Express the feelings associated with the abuse. (16, 17, 18, 19)

9. Identify the impact of the abuse upon social functioning. (20, 21, 22)

10. Participate in a support group for abused children. (23)

11. Participate in systematic desensitization. (24)

12. Practice relaxation techniques. (25)

13. Report an absence of intrusive memories, nightmares, and fear. (24, 25, 26, 27)

the same level as the child (e.g., sitting on the floor).

2. Utilize age-appropriate interview strategies (e.g., use of toys and dolls) to establish rapport.

3. Complete a psychosocial assessment, focusing on sexual practices of the parents, privacy (or the lack of privacy) utilized in the home, recent sex education in school, extent of sexual education offered in the home.

4. Obtain accurate corroboration of the traumatic event through collecting collateral information from child protective services, siblings, neighbors, teachers, and any written materials (e.g., child abuse investigation reports, medical reports, police reports, etc.).

5. Coordinate a child abuse assessment with law enforcement or child protective services to prevent further traumatization and/or manufactured memories caused by multiple inquiries about the abuse.

6. Explain to the child that you must notify appropriate authorities (e.g., law enforcement, child protective services, etc.) regarding suspected abuse of him/her. Inquire as to the results of their investigation.

7. Using anatomically correct dolls or drawn outlines of the human body, ask the

14. Parents receive and cooperate with treatment. (28, 29, 30, 31)

15. Parents attend support and/or psychotherapy group for abusive parents. (29, 30)

16. Parents attend parenting classes. (31)

17. Parents verbalize an increased understanding of appropriate discipline methods. (31, 32, 34)

18. Parents identify social stressors that are contributing to loss of control when angry. (33, 34)

19. Parents utilize community resources to assist in resolving psychosocial stressors. (29, 30, 31, 35, 36)

20. Parents identify childhood experiences that taught him/her that abusive behavior is to be expected, excused, and tolerated. (29, 30, 37, 38, 39)

21. Parents draw a genogram depicting a family history of violence and/or incest. (39)

22. The perpetrator verbalizes responsibility for the abuse. (40, 41)

23. The parent apologizes for the abuse. (41)

24. Cease assuming responsibility for the abuse and places blame on the perpetrator. (40, 41, 42)

25. Parents verbalize an increased understanding of

child how he/she refers to his/her genitals and other body parts on the doll's body.

8. Request that the child be placed in protective custody (e.g., pediatric unit of the hospital, group home, foster care, etc.).

9. Determine that the abusive parent does not have contact with the child.

10. Inquire as to the child's and other household members' safety in each session. Report any abuse to the appropriate authorities.

11. Determine who has legal authority to authorize treatment of the child (child protective services, parents, foster parents, etc.), and obtain permission to treat the child for emotional and psychological consequences of abuse.

12. Refer the child to a pediatrician for an evaluation of any injuries, and monitor the caregiver's compliance with the assessment and treatment recommendations.

13. Refer the child to a pediatrician who is trained to conduct child sexual abuse examinations for evidence collection through the use of a rape kit.

14. Obtain releases of information from the identified responsible party, and contact the child's teacher to in-

the appropriate boundaries between family members. (29, 30, 38, 43)

—. _____
_____

—. _____
_____

—. _____
_____

quire about the child's behavior in school.

15. Notify the school of recent events, and encourage their cooperation in identification of emotional distress.

16. Utilize assessment scales to assess the mental status of the child [e.g., the Reynolds Child Depression Scale, the Symptom Checklist 90, or the Trauma Symptom Checklist for Children (Briere)].

17. Encourage the expression of emotions (fear, betrayal, rage, etc.) regarding the abuse.

18. Establish a rapport with the child with a parent present, and then meet with the child alone to further assess the abuse allegation and allow expression by the child without parental influence.

19. Utilize play therapy techniques to assist the child in expressing emotional reactions to the abuse.

20. Explore the child's sociability and self-confidence since the abuse.

21. Teach and reinforce the child's need to accept and think positively about himself/herself rather than define himself/herself as bad because of the bad things that were done to him/her.

22. Encourage the child to reach out to peers with self-

confidence; use role playing and modeling to teach social skills.

23. Refer the child to a support group for abused children.

24. Have the child describe in graphic detail (e.g., sounds, sights, smells, emotions, touch/physical contact, etc.) their memories of the abuse. Begin with the least anxiety-provoking memories to assist with desensitization.

25. Teach the child relaxation techniques: deep-breathing exercises, progressive muscle relaxation, cue-controlled relaxation, and differential relaxation.

26. Monitor the child for signs and symptoms of acute and/or posttraumatic stress disorder. Treat accordingly. [See the chapters entitled "Posttraumatic Stress Disorder (PTSD)" and/or "Acute Stress Disorder" of this Planner].

27. Role-play with the child fear-producing situations and utilize relaxation techniques to cope with anxiety that is precipitated by the experience; encourage the child to practice this skill in real-life situations.

28. Collaborate with child protective services by ascertaining their plans regarding long-term custody of the child and treat-

ment recommended for the parents. Monitor the parents' compliance with recommendations and notify child protective services of any noncompliance.

29. Require that the parents attend a psychotherapy group for abusive parents.

30. Refer the parents to a support group that will assist them in developing skills necessary to establish and maintain safety of the child such as Parents Anonymous, Parents United, or some similar group.

31. Refer the parents to parenting classes. Monitor their attendance by contacting the group facilitator. Confront the parents with any absences and/or notify the appropriate authorities.

32. Educate the parents on nonviolent discipline methods such as time-outs, removing privileges, and immediate consequences for undesired behaviors before they escalate.

33. Assist the parents in identifying any social stressors such as limited finances, isolation, or problems with housing that are contributing to the abuse in the home.

34. Educate the parents on anger management techniques (walking away, taking a deep breath, counting

to 10, hugs-versus-hits philosophy) so as not to discipline their child when the parents are enraged/angered.

35. Educate the parents about community resources [housing programs, Aid to Families with Dependent Children (AFDC), Women with Infants and Children (WIC), etc.] that can assist in resolving social stressors.

36. Refer the parents to the local welfare department to identify programs for which they are eligible.

37. Inquire if the parent was abused during childhood, or witnessed abuse between her/his parents. Discuss how this has contributed to perpetrating abuse against their own child.

38. Assist the parents in identifying childhood events that taught them to excuse abusive behavior; teach appropriate limits and boundaries for behavior.

39. Assist the parents in drawing a genogram with notations indicating each relationship that contained emotional, verbal, and/or physical abuse, as well as sexual abuse and/or incest.

40. Conduct a family session where the child confronts the perpetrator with the abuse and its emotional and psychological consequences.

Confront the perpetrator with the facts through the use of medical reports and the child's statements when he/she is minimizing or denying any aspect of the abuse.

41. Conduct a family session where the perpetrating parent apologizes for the abuse and agrees to a plan to prevent its recurrence.

42. When the child expresses guilt/self-blame, redirect him/her to view the event as something that happened beyond his/her control, placing the blame on the perpetrator.

43. Assist the parent in identifying and implementing changes (respecting privacy by closing doors, stopping any overt sexual behavior in front of the child, etc.) in the household that honor emotional, physical, and sexual boundaries.

__. _____
   _____

__. _____
   _____

__. _____
   _____

DIAGNOSTIC SUGGESTIONS

Axis I:	308.3	Acute Stress Disorder
	309.xx	Adjustment Disorder
	995.5	Neglect of Child (Victim)
	307.47	Nightmare Disorder
	313.81	Oppositional Defiant Disorder
	995.5	Physical Abuse of Child (Victim)
	309.81	Posttraumatic Stress Disorder
	309.21	Separation Anxiety Disorder
	995.5	Sexual Abuse of Child (Victim)
	_____	_____
	_____	_____
Axis II:		
	V71.09	No Diagnosis
	_____	_____
	_____	_____

CRIME VICTIM TRAUMA

BEHAVIORAL DEFINITIONS

1. Exposure to a crime that involved death to someone else, actual or threatened death or serious injury to self (e.g., kidnapping, carjacking, home invasion/burglary, assault) or workplace crisis (robbery, hostage, bomb threat).
2. Subjective experience of intense fear, helplessness, or horror.
3. Recurrent, intrusive, traumatic memories, flashbacks, nightmares, and/or hallucinations related to crime.
4. Intense psychological distress during exposure to events, places, or people that are reminders of the crime.
5. Symptoms of increased arousal such as difficulty sleeping, irritability, poor concentration, hypervigilance, exaggerated startle response, motor restlessness, easily enraged, and/or frequent outbursts of anger.
6. Difficulty concentrating, anhedonia, and/or detachment or estrangement from others.
7. Physical symptoms of chest pain, chest pressure, sweats, shortness of breath, headaches, muscle tension, intestinal upset, heart palpitations, or dry mouth.

__. _____
   _____
   _____

__. _____
   _____
   _____

__. _____
   _____

LONG-TERM GOALS

1. Elimination of intrusive memories, nightmares, flashbacks, and hallucinations.
2. Assimilate the crime experience into life without ongoing distress.
3. Return to the levels of occupational, psychological, and social functioning that were present before the crime took place.
4. Feel empowered in daily functioning with a restored sense of dignity and an increased feeling of personal security.
5. Confront, forgive, or accept the perpetrator of the crime.

—. _____
   _____
   _____
—. _____
   _____
   _____
—. _____
   _____

SHORT-TERM OBJECTIVES

1. Receive medical care for any injury that has resulted from the trauma. (1, 2)
2. File a report with law enforcement. (3)
3. Recall the details of the crime accurately and without cognitive distortions or emotional devastation. (4, 5, 6, 7, 19)
4. Describe the emotional reaction at the time of the crime taking place. (8, 9)
5. Describe the emotional reactions experienced since the crime was committed. (10, 11, 12)
6. Cooperate with psychological testing to determine the

THERAPEUTIC INTERVENTIONS

1. Assist in getting the person to an urgent care or emergency department for medical consultation.
2. Refer the client to a physician for a medical evaluation and treatment.
3. Refer the client to a local law enforcement agency to file a report of the crime.
4. Ask the client to carefully recall all the details of the crime verbally and/or in writing.
5. Consult with law enforcement, relatives, or coworkers who have facts and/or details regarding the crime, to corroborate and/or elaborate on the client's recall.

severity of the impact of the crime. (11)

7. Describe the impact the crime has had upon personal, social, occupational, and daily functioning. (11, 13, 14, 15)

8. Report an increased sense of control. (16, 17, 18, 19)

9. Report an absence of intrusive thoughts, memories, and/or flashbacks. (20, 21)

10. Participate in eye movement desensitization and reprocessing (EMDR). (21)

11. Verbalize an increased understanding of the role of anger and how to manage it. (22, 23)

12. Practice relaxation techniques when feeling anxious or threatened. (24, 25)

13. Identify people who can be relied upon for social support. (26, 27)

14. Report an increased feeling of safety and security in the home. (28, 29)

15. Stop looking for the perpetrator in society. (30, 31)

16. Place responsibility for the trauma on the perpetrator without equivocation. (32, 33, 34)

17. Verbalize an understanding of the psychological benefits and the process of forgiveness. (35, 36, 37, 38)

18. Confront the perpetrator with the psychosocial conse-

6. Teach the client how to use an automatic thought record to identify and challenge cognitive distortions related to the crime(s).

7. Prompt the client to describe the traumatic experience, noting whether he/she is overwhelmed with emotions.

8. Explore the client's emotional reaction at the time of the trauma.

9. Teach the client how fear inhibits people from fighting back when threatened, and help the client realize that his/her survival was the most important issue.

10. Explore the client's emotional reactions experienced since obtaining physical safety from the crime (i.e., fear, revenge, anger, paranoia, etc.).

11. Complete the Trauma Symptom Inventory (Briere), the Beck Depression Scale, or the Symptom Checklist 90 to determine the severity of the impact of the crime.

12. Monitor the client for a persistent mood disorder (e.g., depression or anxiety). (See "Depression" or "Anxiety" in this Planner.)

13. Ask the client to identify how the crime has negatively impacted his/her interaction with friends and family.

quences of victimization. (34, 37, 38)

19. Receive services from a victim witness program to assist with emotional and financial support. (39)

20. Participate in court proceedings. (37, 38, 40)

21. Verbalize emotional reactions to the perpetrator's release from jail/prison. (41)

—.

—. _____

—. _____

14. Ask the client to make a list of the ways the crime(s) has impacted his/her life and to process this list with the therapist.

15. Assess ways in which the client feels vulnerable in his/her home, car, job, and relationships.

16. Train the client in assertiveness skills to increase his/her sense of control and decrease feelings of vulnerability.

17. Explore whether the client feels a loss of control over his/her emotions. Identify ways to recapture that control through use of journaling, cognitive restructuring, focused time spent on one particular thought, and so forth.

18. Utilize the therapeutic game Stop, Relax, and Think (Shapiro) to assist the client in developing self-control.

19. Explore distorted cognitive messages that mediate negative emotional reactions to the trauma.

20. Assess and treat the client for intrusive thoughts, memories, flashbacks, and/or nightmares, and so forth. (See "Posttraumatic Stress Disorder (PTSD)" or "Acute Stress Disorder" in this Planner.)

21. Conduct EMDR to reduce anxiety.

22. Interpret anger as a symptom of feeling helpless. Process reactions to interpretations in session.

23. Teach releasing anger physically by hitting a punching bag or pillows; recommend journaling after such an exercise to identify targets of anger.

24. Teach the client relaxation techniques: deep-breathing exercises, progressive muscle relaxation, cue-controlled relaxation, and differential relaxation.

25. Assist the client in developing behavioral coping strategies (i.e., increased social involvement, journaling, physical exercise) that will alleviate the stress reactions.

26. Inquire as to the nature of the client's social support system and encourage him/her to utilize this resource during treatment.

27. Have the client draw an eco-map to graphically depict available social support. Encourage the client to consider a full range of possibilities, including: friends, family, religious leaders, coworkers, neighbors, classmates, and so forth.

28. Walk through the client's home, identifying ways that the home may be made more secure.

29. Review with the client changes that can be made in his/her house, such as installing dead-bolt locks, keeping curtains closed while at home, purchasing a nonstationary phone and/or caller ID, and/or installing a home security system to increase his/her sense of safety.

30. Ask the client if he/she looks at strangers in trying to find the perpetrator. Educate him/her on how this provokes anxiety. Encourage him/her to develop different ways to behave in public, such as avoiding eye contact and practicing relaxation techniques.

31. Utilize a professional sketch artist to compose a drawing of the perpetrator. Remind the client to look at this picture before going into public places to challenge the client's belief that strangers are the perpetrator.

32. Confront the client when he/she takes responsibility for the crime and assist him/her with placing the blame on the perpetrator.

33. Ask the client to verbalize feelings of guilt or shame about not resisting the perpetrator hard enough and allowing the crime to take place.

34. Ask the client to write a letter to the perpetrator that

expresses his/her emotional reactions to the trauma.

35. Recommend that the client read *The Art of Forgiveness* (Smedes) to provide information on the psychological benefits of forgiveness.

36. Teach the healing benefits and the process of forgiveness of anyone who has caused us severe pain.

37. Prepare the client for interaction with the perpetrator by role playing. Assist the client in expressing his/her emotional reactions and direct him/her to begin the forgiveness process.

38. Provide support for the client in a confrontation of the perpetrator. Assist the client in expressing pain, placing responsibility upon the perpetrator, and/or beginning the process of forgiveness.

39. Educate the client on the services available through the victim witness program and refer him/her to the same.

40. Encourage the client to be present during the court proceedings of the perpetrator; process his/her emotional reactions.

41. Prepare the client for emotional reactions related to the perpetrator's release by exploring his/her feelings and thoughts associated with it. Review previously

learned skills and strategies such as assertiveness training and safety precautions.

—. _____

_____

—. _____

_____

—. _____

_____

DIAGNOSTIC SUGGESTIONS

Axis I: 308.3   Acute Stress Disorder
        309.xx   Adjustment Disorder
        296.xx   Bipolar I Disorder
        300.4   Dysthymic Disorder
        300.02   Generalized Anxiety Disorder
        296.xx   Major Depressive Disorder
        309.81   Posttraumatic Stress Disorder

        _____   _____

        _____   _____

Axis II: 301.82   Avoidant Personality Disorder
        301.83   Borderline Personality Disorder
        301.50   Histrionic Personality Disorder

        _____   _____

        _____   _____

CRITICAL INCIDENTS WITH EMERGENCY SERVICE PROVIDERS (ESPs)

BEHAVIORAL DEFINITIONS

1. Serious injury or death of a coworker in the line of duty.
2. Suicide or unexpected death of a coworker.
3. Serious injury or death of a civilian as a result of emergency service activity.
4. Subjective experience of distress after providing emergency services to a relative, friend, or coworker.
5. Serious injury, death, and/or violence to a child.
6. Death of a patient following prolonged rescue attempts/heroic efforts.
7. Rescue incident attracting unusually extensive media attention.
8. Multiple fatalities or a mass-casualty incident.
9. Shooting of a subject; suicide of a subject in custody (e.g., hanging in jail) or use of deadly force.
10. Sense of helplessness, feeling out of control, emotional numbness, needing to avoid contact with others, loss of motivation, feelings of inadequacy and/or guilt.
11. Headaches, nausea, shaking/tremors, fatigue, intestinal upset, diarrhea, increased blood pressure, change in appetite or exhaustion.
12. Experiencing flashbacks, replaying the event over and over in the mind, sense of unreality or disbelief, impaired memory, short attention span, angry thoughts, and/or increased worry.
13. Withdrawing from social, recreational, and/or occupational activities.
14. Increased use of alcohol or drugs.
15. Resistance to communication, or excessive use of "black" humor.

—. _____
_____
—. _____
_____
—. _____
_____

LONG-TERM GOALS

1. Regain control of emotions and return to previous level of functioning.
2. Gain an understanding of the critical incident and its impact upon cognitive, behavioral, physical, and emotional functioning.
3. Reestablish a sense of equilibrium, trust, and hope.
4. Diminish flashbacks, intrusive images, and distressing emotional reactions regarding the critical incident.
5. Regain confidence in ability to perform job duties.

—. _____
_____
—. _____
_____
—. _____
_____

SHORT-TERM OBJECTIVES

1. Verbalize current emotional reactions to the incident. (1, 2, 3)
2. Verbalize an understanding that emotional reactions are a normal response to the incident. (2, 3)
3. Participate in a critical incident stress debriefing. (4, 5, 6)

THERAPEUTIC INTERVENTIONS

1. Explore the client's emotional reactions following the incident.
2. Encourage and facilitate sharing by the client with a professional peer of the client's to validate the normalcy of his/her emotions experienced.

4. Identify any bodily injury or physical symptoms that resulted from the incident and receive medical care for the same. (7)

5. Describe the facts of the incident, recalling information experienced through all of his/her senses (sight, smell, touch, etc.). (6, 8, 9, 10)

6. Describe the emotions that were experienced at the time of the incident. (11)

7. Identify the aspects of the incident that were most disturbing. (11, 12, 13)

8. Identify the impact that the traumatic event has had upon daily functioning. (14, 15, 16, 17)

9. Verbalize an understanding of the causes of anger related to the incident. (17, 18)

10. Report confidence in and stop second-guessing actions taken during the incident. (19, 20)

11. Report the termination of flashbacks. (21, 22)

12. Increase the frequency and depth of social activity with friends or family. (23, 24, 25, 26)

13. Write a daily social activity schedule. (26)

14. Avoid and/or minimize contact with media, community members, and others who inquire about the incident. (27, 28)

3. Provide written information on critical incident stress reactions to the client for his/her review.

4. Contact a local critical incident stress management (CISM) team to provide a critical incident stress debriefing (CISD).

5. Contact the International Critical Incident Stress Foundation (ICISF) to find a local CISM team.

6. Encourage participation in a CISD that is facilitated by an ICISF-trained debriefer.

7. Inquire as to the medical care that has been received and refer the client to a physician as appropriate.

8. Clarify what the client's role was at the incident.

9. Ask the client to obtain a copy of his/her written report to review the facts of the incident. Identify any cognitive distortions and redirect to more realistic alternatives.

10. Gently ask the client to recall what he/she saw, heard, smelled, and touched while being involved in the incident.

11. Explore the client's emotional reaction at the time of his/her providing emergency services.

12. Ask the client if he/she could change one aspect of the incident without chang-

15. Report adherence to a nutritional dietary plan. (29, 30, 31)

16. Report a reduction of sleep disturbance, distressing dreams, or fear of sleeping. (32, 33)

17. Return to open communication with family, friends, and coworkers. (34, 35)

18. Identify distorted cognitive messages that promote fear, and replace those messages with reality-based self-talk that nurtures confidence and calm. (36, 37)

19. Implement behavioral coping strategies that reduce tension. (38, 39, 40, 41, 42)

20. Attend the funeral of a coworker who has died. (43)

21. Identify cumulative stress reactions. (44)

22. Employ previously healthy stress management strategies to reduce current emotional reactions. (45)

23. Identify the use of alcohol or other substances as a means of coping with stress. (46)

—. _____
   _____

—. _____
   _____

—. _____
   _____

ing the outcome, what would that be.

13. Probe how this incident relates to something in the client's personal life that may be causing a magnification of the emotions.

14. Assess for possible transference of unresolved issues from a previous incident onto this incident.

15. Ask the client to identify how the traumatic event has negatively impacted his/her life.

16. Administer the Trauma Symptom Inventory (Briere) to assess the nature and severity of the emotional, cognitive, and behavioral impact of the trauma.

17. Probe why, at what, and with whom the client is angry; process the anger to resolution.

18. Explore the client's feelings of fear, vulnerability, frustration, or helplessness as causes of angry reactions; encourage acceptance of these feelings as normal rather than becoming angry over them.

19. Ask the client to share his/her thought process before and during the incident that led to his/her actions; reassure him/her of the automatic response that comes with being well trained.

20. Confront the client when he/she negatively evaluates his/her performance during the incident and redirect him/her toward more realistic perceptions by focusing upon the facts of what did take place and his/her professional response.

21. Explore whether the client has had any flashback experiences to this critical incident or previous traumatic events.

22. Determine if the flashbacks are being triggered by something that reminds him/her of the critical incident; explain how flashbacks will diminish as the feelings and facts about the trauma are shared.

23. Educate the client of the psychological consequences of social isolation and encourage him/her to increase his/her level of activity.

24. Encourage the client to attend at least two social events with family or friends.

25. Assist the client in identifying social activities that were a source of pleasure prior to the incident and encourage him/her to resume these activities.

26. Assist the client in writing a daily schedule of events that includes socialization and encourage him/her to follow the schedule.

27. Educate the client about the psychological consequences (e.g., feelings of helplessness, guilt, loss of confidence in rescue work abilities, etc.) of continued exposure to the incident precipitated by contact with reporters, community members, and others who want to discuss the incident; encourage the client to avoid these people.

28. Role-play with the client how he/she will politely respond to those in the community asking questions that he/she does not want to answer.

29. Arrange for the client to have an appointment with a nutritionist. Inquire as to the recommendations and monitor the client's compliance.

30. Encourage the client to avoid caffeine and other foods that stimulate his/her nervous system.

31. Ask the client to keep a log of his/her food intake; encourage eating at regular intervals even though grief may reduce appetite.

32. Assign the client homework of keeping a journal of dreams, nightmares, and disturbing thoughts that are affecting his/her sleep patterns. Process the journal information in session.

33. Process the client's fear of sleeping as possibly a result

of having nightmares or of having to face reality when he/she wakes up.

34. Conduct a conjoint session with the client's spouse/family to facilitate effective communication skills.

35. Encourage the client to talk with peers, supervisors, or his/her spouse about the thoughts and emotions that he/she is experiencing since the incident.

36. Explore the client's distorted cognitive messages that mediate negative emotional reactions to trauma.

37. Help the client develop reality-based cognitive messages that will increase his/her self-confidence and facilitate a reduction in fight-or-flight response.

38. Administer the eye movement desensitization and reprocessing (EMDR) technique to reduce immediate tension.

39. Teach the client relaxation skills utilizing biofeedback techniques.

40. Train the client in progressive muscle relaxation.

41. Train the client in guided imagery techniques to induce relaxation.

42. Encourage the use of strenuous physical exercise alternating with relaxation to alleviate physical stress reactions.

43. Encourage the client to attend the funeral of his/her deceased coworker to facilitate the grieving process. Explore his/her reactions afterward in session.

44. Assess the client for cumulative stress reactions (e.g., chronic fatigue, irritability, or somatic complaints).

45. Explore the client's history of experiencing other traumatic events and determine what coping mechanisms were used to cope with that/those event(s); encourage the use of those healthy strategies again.

46. Complete a substance abuse evaluation and refer the client to substance abuse treatment as appropriate.

___. _____

_____

___. _____

_____

___. _____

_____

DIAGNOSTIC SUGGESTIONS

Axis I:

308.3	Acute Stress Disorder
309.xx	Adjustment Disorder
305.00	Alcohol Abuse
300.4	Dysthymic Disorder
296.2x	Major Depressive Disorder, Single Episode
V65.2	Malingering
304.80	Polysubstance Dependence
309.81	Posttraumatic Stress Disorder
300.81	Somatization Disorder
_____	_____
_____	_____

Axis II:

301.4	Obsessive-Compulsive Personality Disorder
301.9	Personality Disorder NOS
_____	_____
_____	_____

DEPRESSION

BEHAVIORAL DEFINITIONS

1. Depressed, sad, and/or irritable mood.
2. Preoccupation with death, suicide ideation/attempt(s), and morbid themes.
3. Frequent episodes of tearfulness.
4. Change in sleep pattern (insomnia or hypersomnia).
5. Difficulty concentrating and/or completing tasks.
6. Not bathing, showering, and/or brushing teeth on a regular basis.
7. Subjective report of helplessness and/or hopelessness.
8. Decreased appetite and/or weight loss.
9. Decreased social interactions with friends and family.
10. Complaints of lethargy.
11. Mood-congruent hallucinations and/or delusions.
12. Constricted or flat affect.
13. Rumination over past losses (deaths, divorces, separations, etc.) and mistakes.

__. _____
   _____

__. _____
   _____

__. _____
   _____

LONG-TERM GOALS

1. Return to previous level of social and psychological functioning.
2. Express an absence of suicidal ideation and/or urges.

3. Completely grieve losses and initiate interest in new relationships and activities.
4. View life more realistically and optimistically.
5. Enhance and develop new strategies to effectively resolve current conflicts and/or problems.

—. _____
   _____
   _____

—. _____
   _____
   _____

—. _____
   _____

SHORT-TERM OBJECTIVES

1. Cooperate with a comprehensive biopsychosocial assessment. (1)
2. Describe the severity of the depressed mood. (1, 2, 3)
3. Participate in a psychiatric evaluation. (4, 5)
4. Take antidepressant medication as prescribed. (5)
5. Identify the current stressors contributing to the depressed mood. (6, 7)
6. Verbalize any thoughts of suicide. (8)
7. Write a contract agreeing not to harm self and agree to contact a therapist or crisis line when feeling suicidal urges. (9)
8. Cooperate with psychiatric hospitalization (or partial hospitalization) until able to genuinely contract not to harm self. (10)

THERAPEUTIC INTERVENTIONS

1. Conduct a comprehensive biopsychosocial assessment including previous episodes of depression, history of psychiatric hospitalizations and suicide attempts, recent and distant losses, and the length and severity of current depressive episode.
2. Administer the Beck Depression Inventory.
3. Assist the client in scaling his/her depression from 1 to 10, with 10 being a severely debilitating, suicidal depression.
4. Refer the client to a psychiatrist or physician for a psychotropic medication evaluation.
5. Inquire into the client's compliance with and the effectiveness of the prescribed medication, and reinforce

9. Identify sources that can provide emotional support during any crisis. (11, 12)

10. Utilize religious support during the crisis. (11, 12, 13, 14)

11. Identify times when depression was successfully averted. (15)

12. List pleasurable activities. (16, 18)

13. Increase overall social, vocational, recreational, and household duty activity. (17, 18)

14. Identify cognitive distortions that are contributing to depressed mood. (19, 20)

15. Replace distorted, pessimistic, automatic thoughts with more reasonable, optimistic ones. (20, 21)

16. Identify personal goals to mobilize activity and decrease depression. (22)

17. List the actions that need to be taken to resolve the current crisis. (23, 24)

18. Write a plan detailing when and how actions are going to be taken that will assist in resolving the crisis. (23, 25)

19. Verbalize the feelings that are associated with grieving previous losses. (26, 27, 28)

20. Write a letter to the deceased. (28)

21. Verbalize a decrease in depression and an increase in

the necessity of consistently taking the antidepressant.

6. Have the client describe the nature and quality of current relationships, work environment, and other stressors contributing to the depressed mood.

7. Using a narrative therapy approach (see *Narrative Therapy in Practice* by Monk et al.), have the client externalize the problem by naming it ("the blues," "not getting out of bed," etc.).

8. Conduct a suicide assessment, noting details of the plan, backup plans, preparations that were made, perceived control over the impulse, and so forth.

9. Have the client sign a contract agreeing not to harm himself/herself. Detail what actions are to be taken by the client if he/she is experiencing suicidal urges (calling 911, going to the nearest emergency room, calling the therapist, etc.).

10. Refer the client to a more supervised level of care (hospital or partial hospitalization program) if he/she is unable to contract no self-harm to your satisfaction.

11. Inquire about people on whom the client can rely for support (friends, family, religious leaders, coworkers), and encourage him/her to contact them when feeling overwhelmed.

hopeful statements about
the future. (5, 29, 30, 31).

—. _____
    _____
—. _____
    _____
—. _____
    _____

12. Have client draw an eco-
    map (a graphic description
    of relationships with fam-
    ily, friends, coworkers,
    church leaders, etc.) to as-
    sist in identifying sources
    of support.

13. Inquire about the client's re-
    ligious/spiritual beliefs, and
    encourage him/her to use
    this resource for support.

14. Refer the client to a reli-
    gious/pastoral counselor
    commensurate with his/her
    belief system.

15. Using a solution-focused ap-
    proach, ask the client when
    in the last week the depres-
    sion was not as bad, or did
    not exist at all; explore
    what contributed to this
    success, and encourage the
    client to repeat it.

16. Assign homework of identi-
    fying activities that provide
    the client with pleasure.

17. Educate the client about
    how inactivity can deepen
    depression by enabling de-
    structive, self-defeating
    brooding.

18. Encourage the client to in-
    crease the amount of time
    spent in pleasurable and
    constructive activities.

19. Provide the client with an
    automatic thought record
    and ask him/her to list those
    thoughts that are associated
    with the depressed mood.

20. Monitor the use of an auto-
    matic thought record and

assist the client in challenging distorted, negative thinking.

21. Assign the client homework of reading and completing assignments in *Ten Days to Self-Esteem* (Burns).

22. Ask the client the *miracle question* (If your problem was solved overnight, how would you know? What kinds of things would you be doing instead? etc.).

23. Using a narrative therapy (Monk et al.) approach, ask the client what kinds of things he/she needs to do to fight/solve the problem. Encourage him/her to begin these actions.

24. Assist the client in identifying what actions he/she can take to resolve the current crisis.

25. Assign the client homework of detailing what actions will be taken and when they will be taken to resolve the crisis; confront any resistance to the assignment.

26. Probe the client regarding the feelings that are associated with previous losses.

27. Utilizing the Gestalt empty-chair technique, have the client talk to his/her deceased significant other and verbalize the feelings associated with the loss (sadness, anger, betrayal, abandonment, relief, etc). Assist the client in recognizing and ar-

ticulating the negative emotions that may be complicating the grieving process.

28. Assign homework having the client write a letter to the deceased significant other, saying good-bye. Process reactions to the assignment in session.

29. Using the depression scaling method (rating mood from 1 to 10), monitor the client's progress and positively reinforce his/her progress.

30. Have the client repeat taking the Beck Depression Inventory; comparing the client's previous results from the Beck Depression Inventory with current results.

31. Review with the client his/her progress toward goals and confront any negative distortions that arise in session.

___. _____
    _____
___. _____
    _____
___. _____
    _____

DIAGNOSTIC SUGGESTIONS

Axis I: 309.0   Adjustment Disorder with Depressed Mood
             V62.82   Bereavement
             296.xx   Bipolar I Disorder
             296.89   Bipolar II Disorder
             301.13   Cyclothymic Disorder

	300.4	Dysthymic Disorder
	296.2x	Major Depressive Disorder, Single Episode
	296.3x	Major Depressive Disorder, Recurrent
	295.70	Schizoaffective Disorder
	_____	_____
	_____	_____
Axis II:	301.83	Borderline Personality Disorder
	301.50	Histrionic Personality Disorder
	_____	_____
	_____	_____

DISASTER

BEHAVIORAL DEFINITIONS

1. Involvement in a natural disaster (e.g., tornado, flood, hurricane, blizzard, volcano eruption, drought, earthquake, etc.).
2. Involvement in a technological or man-made disaster (e.g., fire, plane crash, or an explosion resulting in the airborne distribution of hazardous chemicals).
3. Involvement in a social/health disaster (e.g., war, economic depression, or health epidemic).
4. Devastation of or extreme disruption to home, community, personal belongings, and/or daily operations.
5. Experiencing a fight-or-flight response of increased adrenaline, sensory acuity, increased heart rate, and/or hyperventilation.
6. Emotional reactions of shock, disbelief, confusion, helplessness, loss of control, irritability, survivor's guilt, anxiety, despair, fear, and/or grief.
7. Physical reactions of sleep and appetite disturbance, exhaustion, dehydration, and/or change in elimination patterns.
8. Clinging, acting out or aggressive behaviors, and regressive behaviors observed in children.
9. Reexperience the disaster in thoughts, dreams, illusions, flashbacks, or recurrent images.
10. Marked avoidance of stimuli that arouse recollections of the disaster, such as thoughts, feelings, conversations, activities, places, or people.

—. _____
   _____

—. _____
   _____

—. _____
   _____

LONG-TERM GOALS

1. Rebuilding of home, community, schools, and/or work environment.
2. Assimilate the disaster into life experience without ongoing distress.
3. Stabilize physical, cognitive, behavioral, and emotional reactions while increasing the ability to function on a daily basis.
4. Diminish the intrusive images and alteration in functioning or activity level that are due to stimuli associated with the disaster.

—. _____
   _____

—. _____
   _____

—. _____
   _____

SHORT-TERM OBJECTIVES

1. Establish shelter and consistently attend to basic needs of food, clothing, hygiene, and sleep. (1, 2, 3, 4)
2. Establish and maintain communication with family members, neighbors, and coworkers. (5, 6)
3. Accept assistance from volunteers. (7, 8, 9)
4. Describe what actions were performed before and during the disaster. (10, 11, 12)
5. Identify the sights, sounds, and physical discomforts endured during the disaster. (11, 12)

THERAPEUTIC INTERVENTIONS

1. Assist the client and his/her family in locating a disaster shelter established by the American Red Cross or another disaster relief organization.
2. Respect the client's need for privacy and private grieving. Offer to make sleeping and identified space in the shelter as personal and comfortable as possible.
3. Encourage the client to eat well-balanced, hot meals as offered through community resources such as the American Red Cross.

6. Obtain medical attention for any physical complaints and/or injuries. (13)

7. Describe the emotional reactions experienced since the disaster. (14, 15, 16)

8. Identify distorted cognitive messages that promote fear and replace those messages with reality-based self-talk that nurtures confidence and calm. (17, 18)

9. Identify the worst part of the disaster. (19)

10. Children share their anxieties and fears. (20, 21)

11. Verbalize an increased understanding of how to meet the family's emotional needs after the disaster. (21, 22, 23)

12. Stop self-blaming for ignoring signals, alarms, and warnings about the approaching disaster. (24, 25, 26)

13. Verbalize an understanding of the cycle of recovery. (27, 28, 29)

14. Attend a critical incident stress debriefing. (30)

15. Identify previously used coping strategies to manage other stressful events in the client's life. (31)

16. Report obtaining a healthy amount of rest/sleep, relaxation, and consuming food regularly. (32, 33)

4. Encourage the client to take naps, rest in between vigorous work, and get a healthy amount of sleep within a 24-hour time period.

5. Utilize the American Red Cross communications hotline or headquarters to provide assistance in locating family members, neighbors, coworkers.

6. Direct the client in ways to keep channels of communication open between family members within the disaster area and with family members from outside of the disaster location.

7. Encourage the client to accept physical and emotional support from loved ones, neighbors, community members, as well as strangers.

8. Reinforce the importance of asking for help from volunteers. Educate the client on how helping others and receiving help from others creates a community of strength and support and positively aids in the long-term recovery from the disaster.

9. Offer assertiveness training that is focused upon asking for help from volunteers and other helpers. Reframe any thoughts of being weak or helpless by reminding the client that everyone would need help in this situation.

17. Implement behavioral coping strategies that reduce stress. (32, 33, 34, 35)

18. Report a decrease in stress and tension. (34, 35, 36)

19. Return to the site of the devastation: home, work, school, and so on. (37)

20. Begin cleaning, sorting through possessions, and rebuilding of home, work, school, and community. (38, 39)

21. Identify social support systems that can assist in long-term recovery from the disaster. (40, 41)

22. Share spiritual beliefs and resources. (42, 43)

23. Prepare for the departure of volunteers, media, and disaster relief.
(40, 41, 44, 45, 46)

24. Identify current situations or experiences (e.g., the sound of alarms, the news reporting on another disaster, etc.) that produce memories or reactions experienced during the disaster. (47, 48)

25. Establish a plan for future disaster preparedness. (49, 50)

__. _____
_____

__. _____
_____

__. _____

10. Sensitively explore the client's recollection of facts about the disaster.

11. Gently ask the client to recall his/her actions taken before, during, and immediately following the disaster, being careful not to press him/her into being overwhelmed.

12. Inquire as to what the client saw, heard, or physically felt when the disaster struck, being careful not to press him/her into being overwhelmed.

13. Make a referral to a physician or the first-aid station for a medical evaluation and assistance.

14. Educate the client that sharing feelings and details of the disaster will assist him/her in recovering from emotional trauma.

15. Explore the client's emotional reactions after the incident.

16. Identify reactions of irritability, fatigue, decreased appetite, decreased sleep, nightmares, sadness, headaches, hyperactivity, decreased concentration, and increased alcohol or drug consumption. Inform the client that these are common reactions to a disaster.

17. Explore the client's distorted cognitive messages that contribute to negative

emotional reactions to the disaster.

18. Help the client develop reality-based cognitive messages that will increase self-confidence and facilitate a reduction in fight-or-flight response.

19. Ask the client if he/she could change one aspect of the disaster without changing the outcome, what would that be; process the response and the causes for it.

20. Reassure and comfort the children in the shelter while their parents are attending to practical matters. Utilize play therapy techniques to assist the children in expressing their anxieties and fears.

21. Assess the children for behavioral/emotional changes, and inform the parent(s) that a wide range of reactions are normal and often transitory including: excessive fear of the dark, social withdrawal, clinging to parents, change in eating and sleeping patterns, aggressiveness, shyness, persistent nightmares, headaches, and/or other physical complaints.

22. Encourage the client to answer the child(ren)'s questions about the disaster, home, school, and future honestly and directly. Inform him/her that it is ap-

propriate to say "I don't know" to unanswerable questions.

23. Assess the client for a preoccupation with protecting loved ones. Encourage the client to allow loved ones personal space and independence.

24. Educate the client that disbelief is a necessary defense that allows people to function.

25. Inquire if the client had a disaster kit in his/her home/work. Reinforce the importance of the seemingly minor actions that the client performed to prepare for the disaster.

26. Confront the client when he/she negatively evaluates his/her actions during the disaster and redirect him/her toward more realistic perceptions by focusing upon the facts of what did take place and a normal response of confusion.

27. Teach the client about the cycle of recovery when surviving a disaster (e.g., heroic phase, honeymoon phase, disillusionment phase, reconstruction phase).

28. Process with the client which phase of recovery he/she is in and ways to effectively work through that phase. (For example, the heroic phase occurs during and immediately after the

disaster, and it is at this time that one is at high risk of personal injury from heroic efforts made for their own and others' safety.)

29. Express the appropriateness of grieving material losses (possessions) as well as the loss of future hopes and plans.

30. Encourage participation in a critical incident stress debriefing that is facilitated by a trained debriefer.

31. Explore the client's history of experiencing other disasters or stressful events, and determine what coping mechanisms were used to cope with that/those events; encourage the use of those healthy strategies again.

32. Encourage the use of strenuous physical activity alternating with relaxation and rest to alleviate physical stress reactions; monitor the client for proper rest and nutrition.

33. Suggest that the client take time for relaxation and recreation. Educate him/her about the importance of taking time away from the work of reconstructing after the disaster.

34. Assist the client in developing behavioral coping strategies (i.e., talking/counseling, journaling, avoiding isolation) that will ameliorate the stress reactions.

35. Administer the eye movement desensitization and reprocessing (EMDR) technique to reduce stress and tension.

36. Teach the client relaxation skills utilizing progressive muscle relaxation or guided imagery techniques.

37. Assist the client in returning to the home/work/school devastated by the disaster. Process the client's reactions to seeing the devastation for the first time.

38. Encourage the client to seek unreplaceable, valued items in the rubble. Educate the client on ways to temporarily preserve those items found (e.g., briefly wash off mud/smoke from the item, store it in a plastic bag, take the sealed bags to a freezer and store in the freezer until time can be taken to restore the item properly).

39. Establish a plan with the client for cleaning, repairing, and/or sorting through their belongings at home, work, or school. Advise him/her not to stop, clean, sort, and reminisce about every item he/she encounters.

40. Educate the client about resources (e.g., American Red Cross, FEMA, etc.) that can assist with providing financial and material support. Encourage him/her to access these resources.

41. Provide the client with a list of people and organizations who can assist in rebuilding his/her home, work, life (i.e., home insurance, banks, federal agencies, relatives, public mental health agencies, etc.); assist the client in adding personal contacts and resources to the list.

42. Explore the client's religious belief system and faith practices; have they changed or been a supportive resource at times of fear and despair?

43. Encourage and facilitate healthy reliance on spiritual resources; direct the client to clergy and religious gatherings.

44. Assist the client in establishing a manageable schedule of activities. Encourage him/her to complete one task at a time to prevent becoming overwhelmed.

45. Assess the client for exhaustion, grief, desperation, and depression that may develop after the media, emergency/volunteer efforts, and attention to the disaster go away. (See the chapters entitled "Depression" and/or "Anxiety" in this Planner.)

46. Encourage the client to keep helping others when the media and the volunteers leave. Educate the client that small acts of

kindness, both received and given, will maintain morale during the process of rebuilding.

47. Assess the client for fear and/or anxiety when the weather conditions are similar to those of the disaster (e.g., high winds, dark clouds, heavy rain, etc.). Encourage the use of coping strategies (e.g., relaxation techniques, positive self-talk, prayers, etc.) learned to manage the distress.

48. Prepare the client for reexperiencing the disaster when sensory memories are stimulated (e.g., the sound of alarms, the news reporting on another disaster, etc.), anniversary dates of the disaster occur, or when media coverage broadcasts the disaster. Encourage the use of healthy coping strategies learned to manage the distress from the memories.

49. Assist the client in developing a disaster plan to increase his/her sense of preparedness and decrease feelings of helplessness. Educate him/her to include in the plan: a meeting location, a checklist of appliances and services to be turned off, and two escape routes out of every room and the residence. Encourage him/her to practice the plan through drills.

50. Assist the client in preparing a disaster supply kit containing three days' supply of water, one change of clothing per person in the household, a blanket and/or sleeping bag, first-aid kit with routine medications, batteries, flashlight, and special items for the elderly or disabled.

__. _____

_____

__. _____

_____

__. _____

_____

DIAGNOSTIC SUGGESTIONS

Axis I:	308.3	Acute Stress Disorder
	309.xx	Adjustment Disorder
	300.02	Generalized Anxiety Disorder
	296.xx	Major Depressive Disorder
	300.21	Panic Disorder with Agoraphobia
	300.01	Panic Disorder without Agoraphobia
	309.81	Posttraumatic Stress Disorder
	307.42	Primary Insomnia
	309.21	Separation Anxiety Disorder
	_____	_____
	_____	_____
Axis II:	301.50	Histrionic Personality Disorder
	301.4	Obsessive-Compulsive Personality Disorder
	_____	_____
	_____	_____

DOMESTIC VIOLENCE

BEHAVIORAL DEFINITIONS

1. Physical assault by spouse/partner (e.g., hitting, slapping, pushing, choking, kicking, etc.).
2. Verbal abuse by spouse/partner (e.g., derogatory comments, name calling, extensive use of profanity, blaming the victim for anything that goes wrong in the relationship, etc.).
3. Emotional or psychological abuse by the spouse/partner (e.g., being stalked, controlled, prohibiting contact with family/support systems, etc.).
4. Sexual assault by spouse/partner (e.g., nonconsensual sexual intercourse, sodomy, forced sexual activity with objects, harming if intercourse is refused, etc.).
5. Self-report of being injured by a spouse or domestic partner coupled with feelings of fear, intimidation, and/or social withdrawal.
6. Bruises, injuries, and/or physical complaints that give evidence of assault.
7. Frequent and prolonged periods of depression, irritability, and/or anxiety.
8. Low self-esteem as evidenced by minimal or no eye contact, frequent self-disparaging and self-blaming statements, and social withdrawal.
9. Avoidance of social activities due to embarrassment concerning physical bruises and other indications of assault.
10. Subjective sense of numbing, detaching, or absence of emotional responsiveness.
11. Avoidance of people and activities that remind self of the abusive relationship.
12. Difficulty sleeping, poor concentration, and/or motor restlessness.

___. _____

_____

—. _____
   _____
—. _____
   _____

LONG-TERM GOALS

1. Develop the skills necessary to maintain physical and emotional safety in current and future relationships.
2. Take legal steps necessary to guarantee safety such as filing a personal restraining order, moving to a safe living situation, and establishing a safety plan.
3. Eliminate all aggression and emotional abuse in the relationship.
4. Eliminate or reduce contact with the abuser.
5. Return to the level of self-confidence as well as emotional and social functioning that were present before the domestic abuse began.
6. Follow through with legal action against the abusive spouse/partner (press charges, testify in court, report harassment, etc.).

—. _____
   _____
—. _____
   _____
—. _____
   _____

SHORT-TERM OBJECTIVES

1. Describe the history, nature, frequency, and duration of abuse. (1, 2, 3)
2. Verbalize the emotional reactions to the abuse. (3, 4)
3. Describe the current degree of safety of all household members. (3, 5, 6)
4. Comply with a comprehensive physical evaluation. (7)

THERAPEUTIC INTERVENTIONS

1. Establish rapport with the client through the use of active listening skills, such as asking open-ended questions, maintaining a nonjudgmental stance, and normalizing emotional reactions.
2. Gather a history of physical, emotional, verbal, or

5. Identify self-blaming behavior for the abusive actions of the partner. (8, 9, 10, 11)

6. Verbalize an understanding that the abuse is the responsibility of the abuser. (9, 10, 11, 12)

7. Report any homicidal thoughts. (13, 14)

8. Describe any role that substance abuse may play in the role of violence. (15, 16)

9. Obtain chemical dependence treatment for own substance abuse problem. (17)

10. Identify the impact of the abuse upon social functioning. (18, 19)

11. Cooperate with a psychological evaluation. (20, 21)

12. Identify those friends and family members who are supportive and willing to get involved in establishing safety. (22, 23, 24)

13. Reveal the details of the physical abuse to a friend or family member. (23, 24)

14. Move to a safe living situation. (6, 24, 25, 26)

15. Write a safety plan that will be implemented to establish and maintain physical safety. (25, 26, 27, 28)

16. Verbalize an understanding of the legal resources available. (29, 30)

17. File a personal restraining order. (30)

18. Cooperate with law enforcement. (31, 32)

sexual abuse that has been endured or witnessed in the current and previous relationships.

3. Speak with the client alone and inquire if he/she has been directly or indirectly threatened to not report the abuse.

4. Explore the client's feelings associated with the abuse, including those of guilt, shame, helplessness, fear, anger, and/or self-blame.

5. Explore whether any other member of the client's current household has also been abused and, if a risk still exists, notify authorities as appropriate.

6. Inquire as to the client's and other household members' safety in each session; if a threat exists, arrange for removal of the perpetrator or escape for household members to a safe living situation.

7. Refer the client to a physician for a physical exam to identify any untreated injuries and to establish evidence that physical abuse has occurred.

8. Explore the client's desire to end the violence but save the relationship.

9. Confront the client about making excuses for the perpetrator's abuse, minimizing its impact, or accepting blame for it.

19. Verbalize an increased understanding of the cycle of domestic violence. (33, 34, 35, 36)

20. Read books/literature on domestic violence. (35)

21. Attend victim support groups. (36)

22. Identify childhood experiences that taught him/her that abusive behavior is to be expected, excused, and tolerated. (37, 38, 39, 40)

23. Draw a genogram depicting family history of violence. (39)

24. Verbalize increased self-confidence. (41, 42)

25. Verbalize ambivalent feelings toward the perpetrator. (43)

26. Verbalize decisions about social activities (e.g., work, living arrangements, friendships, etc.) without reference to being manipulated by the abusing/controlling partner. (44, 45, 46)

27. Seek employment. (47, 48)

28. List behaviors that are potential indicators of impending domestic violence in order to help prevent future episodes. (49)

29. List all behaviors that, if demonstrated by any partner, will result in immediate termination of the relationship. (49, 50)

30. Write a plan for future relationships that includes

10. Confront and challenge any of the client's minimizing regarding the seriousness of the abuse. Assess if the client believes that the perpetrator's remorse means that the abuse will never happen again.

11. Review photographs of the assault, medical reports, and previous history of violence with the client.

12. Explore whether the client rationalizes that something he/she is doing provokes the abuse; consistently point out that abuse is never deserved.

13. Conduct a homicide assessment.

14. Explore the client's feeling homicidal as the ultimate means of freedom and termination of the relationship.

15. Gather a history of alcohol and/or drug use by the client and the perpetrator that occurs before, during, or after violent episodes.

16. Confront minimization by the client of the domestic violence by the abuser because he/she was under the influence of alcohol and/or drugs.

17. Refer the client for chemical dependence treatment, if indicated.

18. Assist the client in identifying the negative impact that the domestic abuse has

safety precautions.
(49, 50, 51)

—. ———————————
———————————

—. ———————————
———————————

—. ———————————
———————————

had on the his/her functioning at work and in social or
family interactions (e.g.,
less productive, withdrawn,
irritable, isolating self, etc.).

19. Assist the client in identifying ways the abuser prohibited relationship building
with support systems (e.g.,
censored mail, prohibited
use of the phone, humili-
ated the client in social/
family functions, etc.).

20. Arrange for psychological
testing (i.e., WAIS-R, Trail
Making, MMPI, etc.) to assist with identifying any
psychopathology and ruling
out any neurological dam-
age from the abuse.

21. Discuss the results of psychological testing, and develop appropriate goals
based on these results.

22. Assist the client in identifying friends and/or family
that would be supportive of
him/her and encourage him/
her to seek their support.

23. Have the client reveal the
severity of his/her abuse to
a friend or family member
to decrease denial and increase social support.

24. In a conjoint session, educate family/friends on ways
they can protect the client,
the need to contact law enforcement, and assess their
own safety.

25. Educate the client about
the availability of domestic

violence or battered women's shelters and other alternate living situations.

26. Assist the client with identifying friends or family who would be willing and able to provide a safe, protected living situation.

27. Develop a written safety plan that details concrete actions (e.g., calling the police, leaving his/her residence, moving to a shelter, etc.) to be taken to establish and maintain physical safety.

28. Develop a strategic plan of not adhering to a daily routine (e.g., encourage leaving/arriving home at different times; use different roadways to travel to/from work/school; have visitors to the house and overnight so to not consistently be home alone).

29. Educate the client about appropriate legal resources (e.g., attorneys, legal aid, victim advocacy programs, etc.), and encourage him/her to utilize them.

30. Discuss with the client the importance of having a personal restraining order in place to assure his/her safety and encourage him/her to file one.

31. Educate the client about the importance of cooperating with law enforcement to prevent future assaults. En-

courage him/her to cooperate with evidence-gathering activities such as photographs of injuries, rape kits, and the like.

32. Refer the client to law enforcement to file a complaint and request increased patrol in his/her neighborhood.

33. Educate the client about the cycle of domestic violence (e.g., tension-building phase; acute battering phase; and the calm, loving phase/honeymoon phase).

34. Educate the client on how the abuser activates the client's hope by expressing remorse, displaying emotional distress, or pleading for forgiveness after the assault.

35. Assign the client homework of reading books on domestic violence, such as *The Battered Woman* (Walker), *Getting Free: You Can End Abuse and Take Back Your Life* (NiCarthy), *Violence Against Women: A Curriculum for Empowerment* (Szymanski), and *The War Against Women: Overcoming Female Abuse* (Ackerman).

36. Refer the client to a domestic violence or battered women's support group.

37. Assist the client in identifying childhood events that taught him/her to excuse violent behavior.

38. Inquire if the client witnessed abuse between his/her parents or other adults in their childhood. Discuss how that experience impacts his/her views on domestic violence.

39. Assist the client in drawing a genogram with notations indicating each relationship that contained emotional and/or physical abuse.

40. Assess religious or cultural beliefs that promote maintaining the marriage or maintaining the façade of a good marriage.

41. Verbally reinforce the client's use of positive statements regarding confidence and accomplishments.

42. Provide assertiveness training to the client, emphasizing the maintenance of physical safety boundaries, and role-play with him/her the application of assertiveness in potentially abusive situations.

43. Encourage the client to talk about his/her ambivalence toward the abuser and toward terminating the relationship; confront unrealistic expectations for change and emphasize his/her need to take responsibility for protecting himself/herself from future abuse.

44. Monitor the client's progress toward increased

social activity, and positively reinforce movement toward that goal.

45. Assist the client in identifying irrational fears regarding being revictimized and replacing those fears with more rational beliefs.

46. Utilizing a solution-focused approach, ask the client what his/her life would look like if the abuse had never happened. Encourage him/her to begin to take the necessary steps to have that life.

47. Refer the client to work training programs or employment opportunities/agencies in order to promote economic independence from the perpetrator.

48. Assist the client in preparing a resume.

49. Review behaviors that are potential indicators of impending domestic violence (e.g., perpetrator's claims of ownership of the battered partner, perpetrator's threats of homicide or suicide, obsessiveness about the partner, possessing or brandishing weapons, etc.). Encourage the client to implement his/her safety plan when such indicators are present.

50. Suggest that the client list all behaviors (e.g., jealousy, controlling, quick commit-

ment, unrealistic expectations, isolation, blaming others, hypersensitivity, animal cruelty, rigid gender roles, property destruction, etc.) that, if present in any partner, would be cause for immediate termination of the relationship.

51. Assist the client with developing a plan for future relationships that includes safety precautions.

—. _____
_____

—. _____
_____

—. _____
_____

DIAGNOSTIC SUGGESTIONS

Axis I:	308.3	Acute Stress Disorder
	309.24	Adjustment Disorder with Anxiety
	309.0	Adjustment Disorder with Depressed Mood
	309.28	Adjustment Disorder with Mixed Anxiety and Depressed Mood
	305.00	Alcohol Abuse
	303.90	Alcohol Dependence
	300.4	Dysthymic Disorder
	296.xx	Major Depressive Disorder
	V61.1	Partner Relational Problem
	995.81	Physical Abuse of an Adult (Victim)
	309.81	Posttraumatic Stress Disorder
	995.81	Sexual Abuse of Adult (Victim)
	_____	_____
	_____	_____
Axis II:	301.82	Avoidant Personality Disorder
	301.83	Borderline Personality Disorder

301.6   Dependent Personality Disorder
301.50   Histrionic Personality Disorder
_____   _____
_____   _____

GENERALIZED ANXIETY DISORDER

BEHAVIORAL DEFINITIONS

1. Excessive anxiety and worry about a number of events or activities that is interfering with daily functioning.
2. Inability to stop or control the worry.
3. Muscle tension, irritability, and/or fatigue.
4. Subjective report of feeling restless or "on edge," difficulty concentrating, or mind going blank.
5. Difficulty falling or staying asleep, or restless, unsatisfying sleep.

—. _____

_____

—. _____

_____

—. _____

_____

LONG-TERM GOALS

1. Develop strategies to induce calm when experiencing anxiety, fear, restlessness, and so forth.
2. Complete normal social, occupational, and/or academic functions.
3. Regain self-confidence, emotional control, and a sense of serenity.

—. _____

_____

—. _____

_____

—. _____

_____

SHORT-TERM OBJECTIVES

1. Cooperate with a comprehensive psychosocial assessment by providing accurate information regarding anxiety, stressors, social support, and history. (1, 2, 3)

2. Identify social stressors that are contributing to anxiety. (2, 3, 4)

3. Verbalize an understanding of how negative childhood experiences have contributed to creating and maintaining anxiety. (5, 9)

4. Identify and cooperate with the treatment of any medical conditions that may be contributing to anxiety. (6)

5. Cooperate with medical evaluation and take psychotropic medications as prescribed. (7)

6. Verbalize an increased understanding of anxiety disorders and their treatment. (8, 9)

7. Verbalize the symptoms of anxiety that are experienced physically, emotionally, and behaviorally. (10, 11)

8. Identify those times when a feeling of loss of control over situations/events in his/her life occurs. (12)

THERAPEUTIC INTERVENTIONS

1. Establish rapport with the client by providing reassurance and warmth.

2. Conduct a comprehensive psychosocial assessment of the client.

3. Have client draw an eco-map (i.e., a graphic description of relationships with family, friends, coworkers, church leaders, etc.) to assist in identifying sources of conflict that may be contributing to anxiety, as well as sources of support.

4. Ask the client to create a list of 10 situations or events that he/she worries about daily for a week. Review with the client situations/events that he/she can change versus those that are out of his/her control.

5. Assist the client in identifying childhood experiences such as overly protective or critical parenting that may have contributed to the onset and maintenance of current anxiety.

6. Refer the client to a physician to identify and treat any medical conditions that may be contributing to anxiety (e.g., hypoglycemia,

9. Identify already-existing anxiety management strategies and increase their use. (13, 14)

10. Design and comply with a nutritional plan that excludes any substances that may exacerbate anxiety. (15, 16)

11. Identify any substance abuse and maintain sobriety during treatment. (17, 18, 19)

12. Utilize community resources that can assist with resolving social stressors that are contributing to anxiety. (20)

13. Practice relaxation techniques. (21, 22, 23)

14. Meditate daily for 15 minutes to decrease the overall level of anxiety. (23)

15. Identify ways in which anger can be discharged appropriately. (24)

16. Demonstrate increased assertiveness in relationships by asking for desired outcomes directly, refusing unwanted requests, and expressing anger openly and appropriately. (25, 26)

17. Increase level of physical exercise. (27, 28)

18. Identify cognitive distortions that are contributing to anxiety. (29, 30)

19. Replace distorted, anxiety-provoking automatic thoughts with more realistic, calming ones. (30, 31)

drug intoxication/withdrawal, parathyroid disease, etc.).

7. Refer the client to a physician for a psychotropic medication evaluation for the treatment of anxiety and sleeplessness; monitor the client's compliance with the physician's orders.

8. Educate the client regarding the genesis (e.g., childhood-learned insecurity, trauma-induced, depression-associated, lack of coping skills, etc.) and treatment (e.g., cognitive coping strategies, behavioral coping strategies, normalization and increased tolerance, medication, etc.) of anxiety disorders. Encourage the client to ask questions and request that he/she repeat the information to demonstrate understanding.

9. Assign the client homework of reading *The Anxiety and Phobia Workbook* (Bourne).

10. Assist the client in identifying his/her symptoms of anxiety and under what circumstances the symptoms are experienced.

11. Ask the client to keep a journal of his/her daily activity and anxiety reactions experienced when engaged in these activities. Review this journal with the client to determine if phobias or

20. Report increased feelings of self-worth and decreased anxiety. (31, 32)

21. List five activities that promote feelings of self-worth. (32)

22. Attend a community support group for people with anxiety disorders. (33)

—. _____
   _____

—. _____
   _____

—. _____
   _____

panic/anxiety attacks are present.

12. Assist the client in determining areas of his/her life over which he/she can exercise control versus those that are out of his/her control.

13. Ask the client to keep a journal of times when the anxiety is successfully managed between sessions to identify coping strategies. Positively reinforce the use of these already-existing strategies.

14. Using a solution-focused approach, ask the client to think about the moments in the last week when he/she did not experience anxiety. Inquire as to what the client was doing during these times, and assign homework of increasing these behaviors.

15. Refer the client to a nutritionist. Request that the client bring the nutritionist's recommendations to the session and monitor compliance with his/her plan.

16. Educate the client on the importance of avoiding stimulants such as caffeine, nicotine, and various over-the-counter medications.

17. Assess the client for any drug and/or alcohol abuse. If present, refrain from treating the anxiety until abstinence has been achieved.

18. Refer the client to a substance abuse program for drug testing on a random basis.

19. Refer the client to a substance abuse treatment program and/or a 12-step group to help establish and maintain sobriety.

20. Refer the client to community resources (e.g., an attorney, financial advisor, etc.) who can assist him/her in resolving external social stressors that are contributing to anxiety.

21. Teach the client relaxation techniques: deep-breathing exercises, progressive muscle relaxation, cue-controlled relaxation, and differential relaxation.

22. Teach the client guided imagery techniques where he/she visualizes a peaceful scene to decrease anxiety.

23. Teach the client meditation techniques and assign homework of practicing meditation for 15 minutes per day.

24. Assist the client in identifying ways to express anger indirectly (e.g., screaming into a pillow, hitting a punching bag, or yelling in private); ask the client to write who or what is the cause of the anger after such a release.

25. Provide assertiveness training to the client, teaching him/her to express feelings

directly, say no, and so forth.

26. Assign the client homework of reading *When I Say No I Feel Guilty* (Smith).

27. Assist the client in designing an exercise schedule and monitor his/her compliance with the routine.

28. Recommend that the client read and implement programs from *Exercising Your Way to Better Mental Health* (Leith).

29. Teach the client to use the Subjective Units of Distress (SUDs) to rank anxiety on a scale of 1 to 10.

30. Teach the client how to use a record of automatic thoughts to identify and track distorted cognitions; challenge and replace the cognitive distortions related to the anxiety.

31. Assign the client homework of reading and completing assignments in *Ten Days to Self-Esteem* (Burns).

32. Assist the client in listing five activities (e.g., challenging cognitive distortions, engaging in physical activity, and socializing with friends and family) that promote feelings of self-worth.

33. Refer the client to a community support group for people with anxiety disorders, such as Phobics Anonymous.

—· _____

_____

—· _____

_____

—· _____

_____

DIAGNOSTIC SUGGESTIONS

Axis I: 308.3   Acute Stress Disorder
309.24   Adjustment Disorder with Anxiety
300.02   Generalized Anxiety Disorder
300.3   Obsessive-Compulsive Disorder
309.81   Posttraumatic Stress Disorder

_____   _____

_____

Axis II: 301.82   Avoidant Personality Disorder
301.83   Borderline Personality Disorder
301.50   Histrionic Personality Disorder

_____   _____

_____   _____

JOB LOSS

BEHAVIORAL DEFINITIONS

1. Elimination of job because of organizational restructuring by the employer (downsizing).
2. Sudden, unexpected termination of employment.
3. Change in physical health (e.g., injury, illness, etc.) that prevents continuing current work duties.
4. Wrongful termination due to discrimination (e.g., sex, age, race, disability, appearance, etc.), or personal conflict with supervisor.
5. Feeling out of control; loss of role identity; emotional numbness; loss of motivation; feelings of helplessness, inadequacy, guilt, or anger.
6. Withdrawing from social, recreational, and/or occupational activities.
7. Symptoms of increased arousal such as difficulty sleeping, irritability, poor concentration, hypervigilance, exaggerated startle response, and motor restlessness.
8. Physical symptoms of chest pain, chest pressure, sweats, shortness of breath, headaches, muscle tension, intestinal upset, heart palpitations, or dry mouth.

__. _____
   _____
__. _____
   _____
__. _____
   _____

LONG-TERM GOALS

1. Develop a long-term plan to meet financial needs.
2. Obtain new employment.
3. Accept job loss and return to previous level of psychological, occupational, and social functioning.

—. _____
   _____
   _____

—. _____
   _____

—. _____
   _____

SHORT-TERM OBJECTIVES

1. Describe, openly and honestly, the situation regarding the loss of employment. (1, 2, 3)

2. Verbalize the emotional reactions to the loss of employment. (2, 3, 4)

3. Report any homicidal ideation. (4)

4. Identify distorted cognitive messages that promote fear and/or hopelessness, and replace those messages with reality-based self-talk that nurtures confidence and calm. (5, 6)

5. Identify any persistent mood disorder. (7)

6. Report a decrease in anger at former employer. (8, 9)

7. Verbalize an increased understanding of the resources available to assist

THERAPEUTIC INTERVENTIONS

1. Build the level of trust with the client through consistent eye contact, unconditional positive regard, and warm acceptance to help increase his/her ability to identify and express feelings.

2. Explore, gently and sensitively, the circumstances surrounding the loss of employment.

3. Explore the client's feelings associated with the loss of employment, including those of guilt, shame, helplessness, fear, anger, and/or self-blame.

4. Conduct a homicide assessment and fulfill duty to warn, if necessary.

5. Explore the client's distorted cognitive messages that contribute to negative

while in financial crisis.
(10, 11, 12)

8. Cooperate with an assessment of employment capabilities and disabilities.
(13, 14)

9. Submit application for social security disability.
(11, 15, 18)

10. Identify people who can be relied upon for social support. (16, 17)

11. Consult with an attorney regarding legal rights related to employment and termination. (18)

12. List the pros and cons of staying in current occupation or field of employment.
(19)

13. Contact vocational rehabilitation services. (20)

14. Read books on the employment search process. (21)

15. Verbalize an increased understanding of the job search process. (21, 22)

16. Identify available employment. (22, 23)

17. Practice job interviewing skills (24, 25)

18. Actively and assertively seek employment. (24, 25, 26, 27)

___. _____

_____

___. _____

_____

___. _____

_____

emotional reactions to the job loss.

6. Help the client develop reality-based cognitive messages that will increase self-confidence and a sense of control over life's circumstances.

7. Monitor the client for a persistent mood disorder (e.g., depression or anxiety), and perform or refer for psychotherapy, if indicated (see the chapters entitled "Depression" or "Anxiety" in this Planner).

8. Interpret anger at employer as a symptom of feeling helpless. Process reactions to the interpretation in session.

9. Teach releasing anger physically by hitting a punching bag or pillows; recommend journaling after such an exercise to identify targets of anger.

10. Refer the client to consumer credit counseling services to obtain information about debt management and to assist in developing a plan to meet financial needs.

11. Provide benefits counseling to the client. Educate about the various state and federal programs (e.g., social security disability, workers' compensation, unemployment insurance, etc.) that may provide assistance and the qualifying criteria for each program.

12. Refer the client to local charities (e.g., Catholic charities, Salvation Army, etc.) that may provide material assistance.

13. Conduct psychological testing to assess the client's ability to engage in gainful employment. Share results with the client in session. Process emotional reactions.

14. Refer the client to a medical doctor/physician to perform an assessment of the client's ability to engage in gainful employment.

15. Assist the client in completing social security disability applications, and advocate for the client during the qualification process.

16. Inquire as to the nature of the client's social support system, and encourage him/her to utilize this resource during treatment.

17. Have the client draw an eco-map to graphically depict available social support. Encourage the client to consider a full range of possibilities, including friends, family, religious leaders, coworkers, neighbors, classmates, and so forth.

18. Refer the client to an attorney specializing in employment law to review reasons for the loss of job and legal options available.

19. Ask the client to list the pros and cons of staying in the current occupation or field of employment.

20. Refer the client to vocational rehabilitation to provide assistance in developing new job skills and determining vocational interests.

21. Suggest that the client read books on searching for jobs (e.g., *What Color Is Your Parachute?* by Bolles).

22. Educate the client on strategies to locate available jobs (e.g., reading the newspaper, job boards, the Internet, visiting the human resources department of potential employers, etc.).

23. Assign the client homework of determining 10 available jobs for which he/she is qualified.

24. Role-play job interviews with the client. Provide feedback regarding his/her attire, appearance, speech patterns, and answers to interview questions.

25. Refer the client to a job coach who can provide assistance with resume preparation, job search, interview skills, and the like.

26. Train the client in assertiveness skills to increase his/her sense of control and decrease feelings of vulnerability.

27. Monitor the client's progress regarding his/her job search. Provide positive reinforcement for all efforts, and discuss any obstacles/setbacks.

___. _____
      _____
      _____

___. _____
      _____
      _____

___. _____
      _____
      _____

DIAGNOSTIC SUGGESTIONS

Axis I: 308.3   Acute Stress Disorder
              309.xx   Adjustment Disorder
              305.00   Alcohol Abuse
              296.2x   Major Depressive Disorder, Single Episode
              V65.2   Malingering
              V62.2   Occupational Problems
              304.80   Polysubstance Dependence

              _____   _____
              _____   _____

Axis II: 301.83   Borderline Personality Disorder
              301.6   Dependent Personality Disorder
              301.9   Personality Disorder NOS

              _____   _____
              _____   _____

MEDICALLY CAUSED DEATH (ADULT)

BEHAVIORAL DEFINITIONS

1. Sudden death of a loved one as a result of cardiac arrest, respiratory arrest, or aneurysm,
2. Death of a loved one following a prolonged illness (i.e., AIDS, cancer, congestive heart failure, etc.).
3. Shock reactions as evidenced by denial, confusion, poor concentration, inability to make decisions, diaphoresis, shaking, or fainting.
4. Affective grief responses of anguish, anxiety, crying, anger, regret, depression, loneliness, and/or abandonment.
5. Cognitive grief response of disbelief, disorganization, preoccupation with the deceased, spiritual confusion, and/or lowered self-esteem.
6. Physical grief responses of agitation, aggressive actions, tightness in throat, heaviness in chest, headaches, and/or diarrhea.
7. Change in social activities, withdrawal from friends known mutually with deceased, lack of contact with associates of the deceased.

__. _____
   _____
   _____
__. _____
   _____
   _____
__. _____
   _____

LONG-TERM GOALS

1. Develop a healthy grieving process following the death of a loved one.
2. Accept the loss realistically, and overcome shock or denial.

3. Return to previous level of social, physical, emotional, and spiritual functioning.
4. Healthy assimilation of this event into the daily functioning of the client(s).

—. _____

_____

—. _____

_____

—. _____

_____

SHORT-TERM OBJECTIVES

1. Verbalize an understanding of the cause(s) of death and the lifesaving attempts that took place. (1, 2, 3)
2. Identify the activities and/ or health of the deceased loved one for the preceding 24 hours. (4, 5)
3. Identify and utilize spiritual sources of support. (6, 7)
4. Receive medical treatment for any physical complaints (i.e., chest pain) in reaction to the death notification. (8)
5. Openly describe all emotional and behavioral reactions experienced. (9, 10, 11)
6. Verbalize an increased understanding of the grief process. (12, 13)
7. Share the grief experience with children. (14)
8. Verbalize a decrease in anger toward medical staff and the deceased. (15, 16, 17)

THERAPEUTIC INTERVENTIONS

1. Establish rapport by maintaining eye contact with the client(s), speaking clearly and slowly, and from the same position (e.g., sitting or standing) as the client(s).
2. Explore with the client(s) what they know of their loved one's condition or events that have taken place. Inform the client(s) that their loved one is dead (using the words *dead* or *died*), and allow for silence following the death notification.
3. Obtain a copy of the medical record. Review the entire report with the client(s), offering pauses to determine how they are absorbing the information.
4. Ask the client(s) to recall the activities/health of the loved one over the past 24 hours.

9. Stop blaming self and/or feeling guilty for the loss. (18, 19)

10. Participate in psychological evaluation and treatment. (20, 21)

11. View the deceased loved one's body. (22, 23, 24)

12. Say good-bye to the loved one. (25, 26, 27)

13. Identify funeral home, burial arrangements, and a memorial service. (28)

14. Decide whether to participate in organ donation. (29, 30)

15. Identify environmental stimuli that trigger grief. (31, 32)

16. Openly share positive and negative memories of the loved one, describing the deceased honestly. (33, 34)

17. Agree to refrain from making major life decisions during this period of intense grief. (35)

18. Agree to avoid making hasty decisions about the loved one's belongings. (36, 37)

19. Decrease the time that is spent daily focused on the loss. (38)

20. Design an activity to be implemented on the anniversary day of the loved one's death or around life events (e.g., birthday, holidays, graduation). (39, 40)

5. Conduct a brief psychosocial assessment to determine the lifestyle, education, values, activities, and such of the loved one. Reflect on this information in a supportive way during the crisis intervention.

6. Inquire about the client's/clients' religious/spiritual beliefs, and encourage them to use this resource for support.

7. Arrange for a clergy or religious leader to visit the client(s) at the hospital, home, site, or some such location.

8. Facilitate the client's (clients') access to emergency medical services or medical personnel as needed for complaints of chest pain or other emergency medical conditions.

9. Normalize the client's (clients') reactions by informing them that a wide range of emotional reactions (e.g., crying, numbness, shock, etc.) are normal, common, and to be expected.

10. Encourage the expression of emotions by asking open-ended questions, providing tissue for tears, and offering reassurance for appropriate reactions.

11. Educate the client(s) that keeping their feelings pent up creates the potential of those feelings only growing

21. Read books on the topic of grief to better understand the experience and increase a sense of hope. (41)

22. Watch videos on the theme of grieving for a loved one, and compare personal experiences with those of characters in the movies. (42)

23. Attend a bereavement support group. (43)

—. _____
    _____

—. _____
    _____

—. _____
    _____

stronger and becoming more destructive with time.

12. Educate the client(s) on the stages of grief (e.g., denial, anger, bargaining, depression, acceptance).

13. Have each client identify where they are in the grieving process and what they wish to do next in their healing (e.g., put up or take down pictures).

14. Encourage the client(s) to openly express their grief reactions with their children to assist them in their own grieving.

15. Gently confront the client(s) regarding any misdirected anger (e.g., toward the medical staff, self, deceased, others). Remind them of anger as a stage of grieving.

16. Interpret anger at the medical staff as a symptom of feeling helpless. Process the reactions to this interpretation in session.

17. Encourage the expression of anger at the deceased. Identify the normalcy of feeling anger at being left alone, the perception that the person lost his/her will to live, and such.

18. Assist the client(s) in identifying and expressing their feeling of survivor guilt.

19. Redirect the client(s) from self-blame by reminding them of the medical reasons for the loss. Refer the

client(s) back to the autopsy report or medical record to validate that there was nothing they could do to change their loved one's death.

20. Conduct a comprehensive mental status evaluation, including previous episodes of mood disorder, history of psychiatric hospitalizations and counseling services, other losses, and severity of current mood disorder.

21. Refer the client(s) to a psychotherapist and monitor compliance with the treatment recommendations. (See the chapters entitled "Depression," "Posttraumatic Stress Disorder (PTSD)," and/or "Acute Stress Disorder" in this Planner.)

22. Inquire from the medical staff as to the appearance of the loved one's body in order to prepare the client(s) psychologically for a viewing.

23. Physically and emotionally support the client(s) in viewing the loved one's body.

24. Educate the client(s) to the fact that viewing the loved one in the environment of his/her death prevents distorted images that may develop in the future about how the loved one died.

25. Encourage the client(s) to talk to the deceased loved

one, share their dreams,
and say good-bye.

26. Assign the client(s) to write
a letter to the loved one,
saying good-bye; include
any unfinished discussions
or disagreements between
self and the deceased. Process their reactions to the
assignment.

27. Utilize symbolic healing
tactics (e.g., sending balloons up in the sky to represent letting go).

28. Encourage active participation in the funeral/memorial
service plans. Discuss the
meaning of each choice (e.g.,
casket, clothing, songs, pall-
bearers, etc.).

29. Educate the client(s) about
organ donation, including
that the loved one's body
will not be disfigured, there
is no cost to the family, and
what organs are viable for
donation.

30. Contact the regional organ
procurement agency for
consent/information on the
donation of the loved one's
organs.

31. Ask the client to bring to a
session the stimuli that remind him/her of the de-
ceased (e.g., smell of cologne,
similar-sounding voice or
laughter of a stranger). Use
desensitization exercises to
diminish intense emotional
reactions when the stimuli
are encountered.

32. Utilize a recording of the deceased's voice or laughter, and process with the client what it is like to hear the deceased again.

33. Assign the client to fold a sheet of paper in half and write the numbers 1 to 10 on each half. Have the client then identify only 10 good traits and only 10 bad traits of the deceased. Process the responses and reaction to completing the assignment.

34. Ask the client(s) to bring to a session yearbooks, degrees, awards, and the like, and have him/her/them share the story behind that achievement of the loved one.

35. Ask the client to share any ideas that he/she is having about starting new relationships, selling a home, relocating, and so forth. Educate him/her on the stress of making major life changes when already under the stress of grieving.

36. Explore the client's need to clean the loved one's room, take care of the belongings, distribute their clothes, and so on. Encourage doing such little by little when he/she is ready.

37. Process the pain that is associated with organizing the loved one's room, boxing up the loved one's belongings, and so on.

38. Establish with the client a quiet time each day when he/she allows himself/herself to think about the death, his/her feelings, and put each into perspective with reality.

39. Explore with the client a ritual that he/she can establish on the loved one's birth date (e.g., going to the grave, having a family meal, etc.).

40. Identify with the client rituals or family traditions, and create new plans involving the loved one's memory.

41. Assign the client to read *When Bad Things Happen to Good People* (Kushner), *Grief, Dying and Death* (Rando), *Living When a Loved One Has Died* (Grollman), or *Getting to the Other Side of Grief: Overcoming the Loss of a Spouse* (Zonnebelt-Smeenge and DeVries).

42. Ask the client to watch films such as *Terms of Endearment, On Golden Pond, Ordinary People,* or similar films that focus on loss and grieving. Discuss with the client how those characters cope with loss and express their grief.

43. Educate the client(s) about community resources such as bereavement groups, Parents without Partners, and Widowed Persons Service.

—. _____

_____

—. _____

_____

—. _____

_____

DIAGNOSTIC SUGGESTIONS

Axis I: 308.3   Acute Stress Disorder

309.xx   Adjustment Disorder

V62.82   Bereavement

296.2x   Major Depressive Disorder, Single Episode

309.21   Separation Anxiety Disorder

_____   _____

Axis II: 301.6   Dependent Personality Disorder

_____   _____

_____   _____

MEDICALLY CAUSED DEATH (CHILD)

BEHAVIORAL DEFINITIONS

1. Sudden death of a child as a result of cardiac arrest, respiratory arrest, aneurysm, or other sudden, unexpected medical condition.
2. Death of a child resulting from sudden infant death syndrome (SIDS).
3. Death following a prolonged illness [e.g., acquired immunodeficiency syndrome (AIDS), cancer, etc.].
4. Shock reactions as evidenced by denial, confusion, poor concentration, inability to make decisions, diaphoresis, shaking, or fainting.
5. Emotional reactions of crying, hysteria, disbelief, or anger.
6. Behavioral reactions of agitation, aggression, tense muscles, clinging to a possession of the child, or social withdrawal.
7. Physical reactions of weakness, fatigue, shortness of breath, loss of appetite, headache, nausea, and/or dizziness.

___. _____

_____

___. _____

_____

_____

___. _____

_____

LONG-TERM GOALS

1. Stabilization of emotional, behavioral, and physical status.
2. Begin a healthy grieving process following the death of a child.
3. Accept the loss realistically, and overcome shock or denial.
4. Return to previous level of social, physical, emotional, and spiritual functioning.

5. Healthy assimilation of this event into the daily functioning of the parents/family.

—. _____

_____

—. _____

_____

—. _____

_____

SHORT-TERM OBJECTIVES

1. Verbalize an understanding that the child has died. (1, 2, 3)

2. Verbalize an understanding of the cause(s) of death and the lifesaving attempts that took place. (4, 5, 6)

3. Identify the activities and/ or health of the deceased child for the preceding 24 hours. (7, 8)

4. Verbalize the lifestyle and hobbies of the child. (8, 9)

5. Obtain social support from neighbors, family members, or friends of the family to prevent isolation after professional staff contact. (10, 11)

6. Identify and utilize spiritual sources of support. (12, 13)

7. Receive medical treatment for any physical complaints (i.e., chest pain) in reaction to the death notification. (14)

THERAPEUTIC INTERVENTIONS

1. Establish a rapport by maintaining eye contact with the parents, speaking clearly and slowly, and from the same position (e.g., sitting or standing) as the parents.

2. Identify who the parents and immediate family are, and congregate them in a secure, private room/area to communicate the death notification.

3. Inform the parents that their child is dead (using the words *dead* or *died*), and allow for silence following the death notification.

4. Explore with the parents/ caretaker what they know of the child's condition or events that have taken place.

5. Obtain a copy of the medical record. Review the entire report with the parents, offering pauses to determine how they are absorbing the information.

8. Abstain from any violent or aggressive behavior. (15, 16, 17)

9. Openly describe all emotional and behavioral reactions experienced. (18, 19, 20)

10. Verbalize an increased understanding of the grief process. (20, 21, 22)

11. Provide emotional support to surviving children. (22, 23)

12. Verbalize an understanding that men and women often grieve in different ways. (24, 25)

13. Verbalize a decrease in anger toward the medical staff. (26, 27)

14. The parents or caretaker will report feeling guilty and stop blaming self for the loss. (28, 29, 30, 31)

15. Verbalize feelings and thoughts about the belief that it is not normal for children to die before their parents. (32, 56, 57)

16. Participate in a psychological evaluation and treatment. (33, 34)

17. View and/or hold the deceased child. (35, 36, 37)

18. Say good-bye to the child. (38, 39, 40)

19. Identify the funeral home, burial arrangements, and memorial service. (41)

6. Assist the parents in obtaining details about life-saving measures from medical professionals and/or paramedics/rescue personnel.

7. Ask the parents to recall the activities/health of the child over the past 24 hours.

8. Ask the parents to share their recent memories of the child.

9. Conduct a brief psychosocial assessment to determine the lifestyle, education, values, activities, and so forth of the child. Reflect on this information in a supportive way during crisis intervention.

10. Assist the parents in making phone calls to nearby relatives/friends to inform them of the child's death; encourage these people to get together with the parents immediately.

11. Hold a family session where the parents and family members share their feelings of grief/loss.

12. Inquire about the parents' religious/spiritual beliefs, and encourage them to use this resource for support.

13. Arrange for a clergy or religious leader to visit the parents at the hospital or home.

14. Facilitate the parents' access to emergency medical services or medical personnel as needed for com-

20. Decide whether to participate in organ donation. (42, 43, 44)

21. Leave the hospital or site within a reasonable amount of time. (45)

22. Share memories of the child openly. (46, 47)

23. Identify the loss of hopes, dreams, and expectations for the child and the family. (48)

24. Begin the process of disposing of the child's belongings. (49, 50)

25. Decrease the time that is spent daily focused on the loss. (51)

26. Design an activity to be implemented on the anniversary day of the child's death or around life events (e.g., birthday, holidays, graduation). (52, 53, 54, 55)

27. Read books on the topic of grief to better understand the experience and increase a sense of hope. (56)

28. Watch videos on the theme of grieving for a child and compare personal experiences with that of characters in the movies. (57)

29. Attend a bereavement support group. (58)

___. _____
    _____

___. _____
    _____

___. _____
    _____

plaints of chest pain, or other emergency medical conditions.

15. Assess the parents for an urge to react violently toward the caretaker, medical staff, or others involved with the child's death, and deescalate verbally.

16. Contact law enforcement or trained individuals who can help behaviorally manage the enraged parents.

17. Notify any intended victims of the parents as mandated by legal requirements.

18. Normalize the parents' reactions by informing them that a wide range of emotional reactions (crying, numbness, shock, etc.) are normal, common, and to be expected.

19. Encourage the expression of emotions by asking open-ended questions, providing tissue for tears, and offering reassurance that all reactions are appropriate.

20. Educate the parents that keeping their feelings pent up has the potential of only making them grow stronger and becoming more destructive with time.

21. Educate the parents on the stages of grief (e.g., denial, anger, bargaining, depression, acceptance).

22. Encourage the parents to share their emotional reac-

tions with their surviving children.

23. Educate the parents about the ways children grieve at different ages and the ways parents can be supportive. Ask the parents to identify the grief reactions they see in their children.

24. Educate the parents to the fact that men and women often grieve in different ways, to increase their understanding of each other and normalize their differences. Teach them that men often repress their emotions, whereas women are more outwardly expressive. Assign the parents to read *Men Are from Mars, Women Are from Venus* (Gray) to normalize the gender differences in grieving.

25. Have each parent identify where they are in the grieving process and what they wish to do next in their healing (e.g., put up or take down pictures).

26. Gently confront the parents regarding any misdirected anger (e.g., toward the medical staff, self, caretakers, others, etc.). Remind them of the stages of grieving.

27. Interpret anger at the medical staff as a symptom of feeling helpless. Process reactions to this interpretation in session.

28. Assist the parents in identifying and expressing their feeling of survivor guilt.

29. Refer the parents to the autopsy report or medical record to validate that there was nothing they could have done to change their child's death.

30. Explore with the parents their regrets by asking about what they believe they could have, should have, or would have done to prolong their child's life. Redirect them to focus on the facts surrounding their child's death, and educate them that ruminating over "what if's" is perpetuating their feelings of guilt.

31. Redirect the parents/caretaker from self-blame by reminding them of the medical reasons for the loss.

32. Explore the feelings and thoughts associated with the belief that it is not normal to have children die before the parents/grandparents.

33. Conduct a comprehensive mental status evaluation, including previous episodes of mood disorder, history of psychiatric hospitalizations and counseling services, other losses, and severity of current mood disorder.

34. Refer the parents to a psychologist or social worker and monitor their compli-

ance with treatment recommendations. (See the chapters entitled "Depression," "Posttraumatic Stress Disorder (PTSD)," and/or "Acute Stress Disorder" in this Planner.)

35. Inquire from the medical staff as to the appearance of the child's body to prepare the parents psychologically.

36. Physically and emotionally support the parents in viewing and/or holding the child's body.

37. Educate the parents that viewing the child in the environment of his/her death prevents distorted images that may develop in the future about how the child died.

38. Utilize symbolic healing tactics (e.g., sending balloons up in the sky to represent letting go).

39. Encourage the parents to talk to the child, share their dreams, and say good-bye.

40. Assign the parents to write a letter to the child, saying good-bye. Process their reactions to the assignment.

41. Facilitate the parents in making decisions and arrangements related to funeral home selection, crematorium, burial, and/or a memorial service.

42. Educate the parents about organ donation, including that the child's body will

not be disfigured, there is no cost to the family, and what organs are viable for donation.

43. Inquire about any religious or psychological objections to organ donation.

44. Contact the regional organ procurement agency for consent/information on the donation of the child's organs.

45. Using a solution-focused approach, ask the parents how they will know when it is time to leave their deceased child and return home. Assist them in completing any tasks that prevent them from leaving comfortably.

46. Using a special photo album, have the parents create a creative memory album or dedication to the child through use of photos.

47. Ask the parents to bring to a session yearbooks, degrees, awards, and such, and have the parents share the story behind that achievement of the child's.

48. Explore what future plans were imagined for the child and the family; empathize with the lost dreams.

49. Explore the parents' need to clean their child's room, take care of the belongings, distribute the clothes, and so forth. Encourage them to perform these functions gradually to avoid feeling

overwhelmed or regretting decisions that cannot be reversed.

50. Process the pain associated with organizing their child's room, boxing up their child's belongings, and so forth.

51. Suggest that the parents set aside a specific time-limited period each day to focus on mourning the loss (e.g., 20 minutes each morning). After the time period is up, the parents will go on with their regular daily activities with an understanding that they will put aside the mourning feelings that occur throughout the day until the next scheduled time.

52. Explore with the parents a ritual that they can establish on the child's birth date.

53. Explore with the parents ways they might participate in their child's graduation class service (e.g., having a flower on the podium, name in the program, moment of silence, etc.).

54. Encourage the parents to use the money that would have been spent on a gift for the child to purchase something special for someone (or a child's organization) of whom the child was fond.

55. Identify with the parents' rituals or family traditions, and create new plans involving the child's memory (e.g., visiting the grave, vol-

unteering on a pediatric
unit at a hospital, etc.).

56. Assign the parents to read
    *When Bad Things Happen
    to Good People* (Kushner),
    The Bereaved Parent
    (Schiff), *A Child Dies: A
    Portrait of Family Grief*
    (Hagan Arnold), *Grief,
    Dying and Death* (Rando),
    or *Living When a Loved One
    Has Died* (Grollman).

57. Ask the parents to watch
    films that focus on loss and
    grieving (e.g., *Ordinary Peo-
    ple*). Discuss with the par-
    ents how those characters
    cope with loss and express
    their grief.

58. Educate the parents about
    community resources such
    as Compassionate Friends,
    SIDS support groups, be-
    reaved parents support
    groups, and so on.

—. _____
   _____

—. _____
   _____

—. _____
   _____

DIAGNOSTIC SUGGESTIONS

Axis I: 308.3   Acute Stress Disorder
           309.xx   Adjustment Disorder
           V62.82   Bereavement
           296.2x   Major Depressive Disorder, Single Episode

	300.21	Panic Disorder without Agoraphobia
	309.21	Separation Anxiety Disorder
	_____	_____
	_____	_____
Axis II:	301.6	Dependent Personality Disorder
	301.9	Personality Disorder NOS
	_____	_____
	_____	_____

MISCARRIAGE/STILLBIRTH/ ABORTION

BEHAVIORAL DEFINITIONS

1. Spontaneous termination of pregnancy by natural causes before 20 weeks of pregnancy.
2. Child born without life after 20 weeks' gestation and/or weighing greater than 400 grams.
3. Medically induced termination of pregnancy.
4. Grief reactions following the miscarriage/stillbirth/abortion.
5. Severe physical exhaustion, vaginal pain, cramping, heavy bleeding, passing of clots or fetal tissue, heart palpitations, aching arms, and engorged breasts.
6. Decreased social interactions with friends, family, and others.
7. A sense of loss, emptiness, restlessness, helplessness, hopelessness, poor concentration, forgetfulness, and anger.
8. Misunderstanding the causes of miscarriage/stillbirth and/or inappropriately blaming self or the medical staff for the loss.
9. A sense of guilt and regret following an elective abortion.

__. _____
_____

__. _____
_____

__. _____
_____

LONG-TERM GOALS

1. Remember the miscarriage/stillbirth, understand it, accept it, and look forward to the future.
2. Accept that grieving the loss of the child will take longer than other forms of grieving.
3. Understand and accept the intensity and longevity of emotions related to the loss.
4. Return to the previous level of physical, social, and psychological functioning.
5. Develop a sense of peace for the decision to abort the child.

—. _____

_____

—. _____

_____

—. _____

_____

SHORT-TERM OBJECTIVES	THERAPEUTIC INTERVENTIONS
1. Receive appropriate medical care. (1, 2)	1. Inquire as to the medical care that has been received, and refer to a physician as appropriate.
2. Describe the emotions felt after notification that the pregnancy had ended. (3, 4)	2. Ask the client to obtain a copy of the physician's report documenting the treatment of the miscarriage. Review the course of treatment with the client.
3. Name the child in order to assist the grieving process. (5)	
4. Verbalize the grief of lost opportunities for the child and the family. (6)	3. Encourage the client to articulate the emotions related to the termination of the pregnancy.
5. Identify all members of the family who are supportive. (7, 8)	
6. Family members share their grief and client support openly in session. (8)	4. Assign the client to keep a journal of feelings, thoughts, and memories related to the pregnancy.

7. Verbalize an understanding of the medical reasons for the death. (9)

8. Stop blaming self for loss. (10, 11)

9. Verbalize a decrease in anger and blaming toward the medical staff. (9, 12, 13)

10. Identify any questions and/ or misgivings regarding future pregnancies. (9, 14)

11. Verbalize an increased understanding of the grief process. (15, 16, 17, 18)

12. List five actions that will assist with coping with the loss. (18, 19)

13. Exercise to reduce stress and anxiety. (20, 21)

14. Identify nutritional needs, and verbalize a commitment to meet them. (22, 23)

15. Identify and utilize spiritual sources of support. (24, 25)

16. Describe the severity of depressed mood. (26, 27)

17. Participate in treatment for depression. (28)

18. Write a letter to the deceased fetus or child. (29)

19. Create memorabilia of the child to assist with grieving and to commemorate the loss. (30, 31)

20. Verbalize an understanding of the risks and benefits of visiting and/or holding the child. (32, 33)

21. Visit and/or hold the child. (33, 34, 35)

5. Encourage the client to name the child if she has not already done so. Have the client share what name was chosen. Explore why that name had been chosen.

6. Explore what future plans were imagined for the child and the family; empathize with the lost dreams.

7. Create a genogram to graphically depict family structure and the degree of support received from each member.

8. Arrange for the family to be present for a session, and encourage the sharing of their feelings of loss. Validate each member's experience with supportive listening, and reinforce their empathy for the client.

9. Encourage or assist the client in obtaining information about the loss from medical professionals. Ensure that the client has all of her questions answered, including viability of future pregnancies.

10. Redirect the client away from self-blame by reminding her of the medical reasons for the miscarriage/ stillbirth.

11. Ask the client to share the progression of her pregnancy and ways she cared for herself and the fetus; highlight the lack of connection between her behavior

22. Say good-bye to the child. (34, 35)

23. Verbalize an understanding of the possible emotional impact on the projected due date. (36)

24. Role-play how friends, coworkers, and other acquaintances will be told about the loss and how to respond to their potential comments. (37)

25. Identify a funeral home, make burial arrangements, and create a memorial service. (38, 39)

26. Identify own criteria for successfully coping with grief. (40)

27. Identify ongoing sources of support during the grief process. (41)

28. Attend a support group for parents who experienced a miscarriage or stillbirth. (42)

29. Express guilt or ambivalence related to having elected to have an abortion. (43)

30. Describe the factors that led to the abortion decision. (44)

31. Verbalize a need for forgiveness and the steps to obtain it. (45, 46, 47)

32. Report successfully asserting self to set limits on those who try to induce guilt. (48)

___. _____
_____

and the miscarriage/stillbirth.

12. Gently confront the client regarding any misdirected anger. Remind the client of the stages of grieving in which anger is a common component.

13. Interpret anger at medical staff as a symptom of the client's feeling helpless. Process the reactions to this interpretation in session.

14. Encourage the client to explore the criteria for both physical and emotional readiness for attempting future pregnancies.

15. Educate the client on the stages of grief (e.g., denial, anger, bargaining, depression, acceptance).

16. Educate the client that keeping feelings pent up has the potential of strengthening the emotions and their becoming more destructive with time.

17. Reassure the client that grief is personal and that everyone differs in the way that it is processed.

18. Provide the client with a list of books that provide information about grief and miscarriage/stillborn births (e.g., Ilse's *Empty Arms: A Guide to Help Parents and Loved Ones Cope with Miscarriage, Stillbirth, and Newborn Death* and *Miscarriage: A Shattered Dream,*

__.　_____
　　　_____

__.　_____
　　　_____

Schiff's *The Bereaved Parent,* and Kubler-Ross's *On Death and Dying*).

19. Educate the client about various strategies that may assist in coping with loss (e.g., journaling, reading literature on miscarriage/ stillbirths, meditation, or getting enough sleep).

20. Encourage the client to exercise nonvigorously (e.g., brisk walks).

21. Recommend that the client read and implement programs from *Exercising Your Way to Better Mental Health* (Leith).

22. Educate the client on the need for a well-balanced diet that is high in bulk, protein, and vitamins.

23. Assist the client in obtaining a dietary consultation.

24. Inquire about the client's religious/spiritual beliefs, and encourage her to use this resource for support.

25. Reinforce the client, using faith as a source of comfort, not a source or cause of the miscarriage/stillbirth.

26. Conduct a comprehensive mental status evaluation that includes an assessment of previous episodes of mood disorder, history of psychiatric hospitalizations and counseling services, other losses, and severity of current moods.

27. Conduct psychological testing (e.g., MMPI-2, SCL-90, Beck Depression Inventory, etc.) to identify the severity of depressed mood.

28. Refer the client to a psychiatrist or psychologist, and monitor compliance with treatment recommendations. (See the chapter entitled "Depression" in this Planner).

29. Assign the client to write a letter to her deceased fetus or child, saying good-bye. Process the client's reaction to the assignment.

30. Assist the client in obtaining mementos of the child (e.g., a lock of hair, a set of footprints, a birth certificate, a picture of the child, the plastic arm identification band from the hospital, a small scrap of paper from the fetal monitoring device, or a record of the child's weight, length, and head and chest measurements).

31. Encourage the client to take photographs or obtain a print of the sonogram of the child (as possible) to keep as mementos. Remind the client to write on a piece of paper what each picture is actually of (positions of child/fetus, etc.).

32. Inform the client that viewing the child now will assist in preventing distorted images that might occur without viewing.

33. Have medical staff explain to the client how the child will look prior to the visit.

34. Encourage the client to hold, talk to, share dreams, and say good-bye to the child or to the ultrasound print.

35. Encourage holding the child in a special blanket, a special outfit, or with a Bible or book purchased for the child.

36. Educate the client about the possibility of a reemergence of grief reactions on the projected due date.

37. Have the client role-play how she will inform others of her loss. Assist the client in anticipating difficult situations by asking "dumb" questions and making comments to desensitize the client's reaction.

38. Encourage the client to actively participate in funeral/memorial plans. Ask the client to identify a funeral home, church, or crematorium.

39. Encourage the client to actively participate in planning and implementing a memorial service for the child. Process the client's reactions.

40. Using a solution-focused approach, ask the client how she will know when she can cope with the grief sufficiently to carry on necessary daily activities. What

will be the behavioral indications?

41. Remind the client that grieving will continue at various levels of intensity for some months, and assist her in identifying sources of support (e.g., clergy, parent, sibling, counselor, friend, support group, etc.).

42. Refer the client to a support group for parents who have experienced a miscarriage or stillbirth.

43. Explore the feelings of guilt or ambivalence related to the abortion decision.

44. Explore the factors that contributed to the abortion decision, and express empathy for those pressures.

45. Teach the steps of the forgiveness process, and assist the client in identifying the sources of forgiveness for the abortion that are relevant to her (e.g., herself, God, father of the child, parents, etc.).

46. Assist the client in identifying to whom she is realistically accountable for her abortion decision.

47. Emphasize the forgiveness we all need from time to time when we compromise our own values.

48. Explore whether there are outside sources of guilt induction pressuring the client (e.g., parents, clergy, friends, etc.), and identify

assertive techniques for setting boundaries between
the client and others.

—.   _____

     _____

—.   _____

     _____

—.   _____

     _____

DIAGNOSTIC SUGGESTIONS

Axis I: 308.3   Acute Stress Disorder
              309.0   Adjustment Disorder with Depressed Mood
              V62.82   Bereavement
              296.2x   Major Depressive Disorder, Single Episode

              _____   _____

              _____

Axis II: 301.6   Dependent Personality Disorder

              _____   _____

              _____   _____

PHOBIAS

BEHAVIORAL DEFINITIONS

1. Marked and persistent fear that is excessive and unreasonable, cued by the presence or anticipation of a specific object or situation (e.g., height, flying, insect/animal, bridge, needle, etc.).
2. The avoidance, anxious anticipation, or distress of the feared situation(s) interferes significantly with a daily routine, occupational (or academic) functioning, social activities, and/or relationships.
3. Physical symptoms of nausea, excessive perspiration, shallow breathing, and/or accelerated heart rate occur when confronting the feared object or situation.
4. Avoidance of the feared situation.
5. Subjective experience of intense anxiety when the phobic situation is confronted and/or contemplated.
6. The phobic fear has developed after experiencing a severe trauma related to the stimulus object or situation.

—. _____
   _____
   _____
—. _____
   _____
   _____
—. _____
   _____

LONG-TERM GOALS

1. Ability to confront the previously feared object, location, or situation without distress.
2. Develop strategies to induce calm when experiencing anxiety, fear, restlessness, and so forth.

3. Ability to complete social, occupational, and/or academic functions without an alteration in daily routine.

—. _____

_____

—. _____

_____

—. _____

_____

SHORT-TERM OBJECTIVES

1. Provide a complete biopsychosocial history. (1, 2)

2. Identify any medical problems that may contribute to impairment or inhibit treatment, and receive adequate medical attention. (3)

3. Comply with an evaluation for psychotropic medication. (4)

4. Take psychotropic medication as prescribed, and report as to its effectiveness and side effects. (5)

5. Identify treatment goals in observable, behavioral terms. (6, 7)

6. Verbalize an increased understanding of phobias and the expectations of treatment. (8, 9)

7. Identify when the phobia started and any traumatic event that is associated with that start. (10, 11, 12)

8. Verbalize physical and emotional anxiety reactions ex-

THERAPEUTIC INTERVENTIONS

1. Establish a rapport with the client by providing reassurance and warmth. Educate the client on the possibility that discussing the phobic situation will cause him/her distress. Reassure the client that the goal of the therapy is to diminish distress.

2. Inquire as to when the client first started experiencing anxiety about the situation/stimulus, and evaluate the phobia's impact upon his/her psychosocial functioning.

3. Refer the client to a physician to identify and treat any medical conditions that may be contributing to anxiety such as hypoglycemia, drug intoxication/withdrawal, parathyroid disease, and so on.

4. Refer the client to a physician for a psychotropic

perienced when faced with the phobic situation. (13, 14)

9. Identify any substance abuse and maintain sobriety during treatment. (15, 16, 17)

10. Abstain from any substances that may be contributing to anxiety. (15, 16, 17, 18, 19)

11. Practice relaxation techniques. (20, 21)

12. Engage in regular, scheduled, physical activity. (22, 23)

13. Challenge cognitive distortions related to the phobia, and replace them with more realistic beliefs. (24, 25)

14. Identify coping strategies that assist with calming anxiety between sessions. (26)

15. Verbalize an understanding of the use of Subjective Units of Distress (SUDs). (27)

16. Participate in systematic desensitization. (28, 29, 30)

17. Participate in eye movement desensitization and reprocessing (EMDR). (31)

18. Identify any secondary gain from maintaining the phobia. (32)

19. Attend a support group for people with phobias. (33)

20. Listen to audiotapes between sessions to assist in generalizing gains and remembering information. (34)

medication evaluation for the treatment of phobic reactions.

5. Monitor the client's compliance with the physician's orders, and assess the medication's effectiveness and side effects.

6. Assist the client in identifying treatment goals in observable terms, such as being able to see the anxiety-provoking stimulus without experiencing panic, reducing the anxiety to levels that do not interrupt daily functioning, and so on.

7. Using a solution-focused approach, ask the client: "How would you know if the problem was miraculously solved?"

8. Educate the client about phobias, including: What causes them? How are they treated? What treatment strategies will be used?

9. Assign the client homework of reading *The Anxiety and Phobia Workbook* by Bourne; process the ideas learned from the reading.

10. Have the client recall the first time that he/she recalls feeling anxiety about the phobic event.

11. Utilize hypnotherapy to help the client recall a traumatic childhood event that is currently provoking the phobia.

21. Write an anxiety management plan to be used after
the termination of therapy.
(35)

—. _____
_____

—. _____
_____

—. _____
_____

12. Explore for any traumatic
event that precipitated the
phobic fear.

13. Inquire if the client experiences symptoms that are
consistent with a panic attack and/or anxiety attack.

14. Ask the client to make a list
of his/her physical, emo-
tional, and behavioral reactions when thinking about
and when confronted with
the phobic situation.

15. Assess the client for any
drug and/or alcohol abuse. If
present, refrain from treating the phobia until abstinence has been achieved.

16. Refer the client to a substance abuse program for
random drug testing.

17. Refer the client to a substance abuse treatment program and/or 12-step group
to establish and maintain
sobriety.

18. Educate the client on the
importance of avoiding
stimulants such as caffeine,
nicotine, and various over-
the-counter medications because of their stimulation
effect on the central nervous system.

19. Refer the client to a nutritionist to learn about a bal-
anced diet and foods to
avoid due to their stimulation effects.

20. Teach the client relaxation
techniques: deep-breathing
exercises, progressive mus-

cle relaxation, cue-controlled relaxation, and differential relaxation; assign daily practice.

21. Teach the client meditation, and assign homework of practicing meditation for 15 minutes per day.

22. Assist the client in designing an exercise schedule, and monitor his/her compliance with the routine.

23. Recommend that the client read and implement programs from *Exercising Your Way to Better Mental Health* (Leith).

24. Teach the client how to use an automatic thought record to identify and track distorted cognitions; challenge and replace the cognitive distortions related to the phobia with realistic, positive thoughts.

25. Monitor the use of the automatic thought record, and assist the client in challenging distorted, anxiety-provoking thinking.

26. Ask the client to keep a journal of times when the anxiety is successfully managed between sessions to identify coping strategies used. Positively reinforce the use of these already-existing strategies.

27. Teach the client to use Subjective Units of Distress (SUD) to rank anxiety on a scale of 1 to 10.

28. Assist the client in creating a hierarchy of his/her anxiety-provoking situations.

29. Using systematic desensitization techniques, encourage the client to imaginally expose himself/herself to the anxiety-provoking situations on the list. Coach him/her to continue to use relaxation techniques to manage anxiety that is rated in SUDs.

30. Assign the client in vivo systematic desensitization between sessions; encourage him/her to use the relaxation technique to manage anxiety during graduated exposure to the stimulus object or situation.

31. Conduct eye movement desensitization and reprocessing (EMDR) to reduce anxiety associated with the phobic stimulus.

32. Assist the client in identifying any secondary gain from maintaining the phobia by asking him/her to describe what he/she will lose when the phobia is gone; explore new, adaptive ways to achieve these rewards.

33. Refer the client to Phobics Anonymous or another support group for people with anxiety.

34. Audiotape sessions and assign homework of listening to the tapes.

35. Review with the client the methods that have worked best to decrease distress, and assign him/her homework of writing a plan to use these methods (utilizing social support, thought stopping, relaxation techniques, etc.) when experiencing symptoms.

___. _____
_____

___. _____
_____

___. _____
_____

DIAGNOSTIC SUGGESTIONS

Axis I:	309.24	Adjustment Disorder with Anxiety
	300.02	Generalized Anxiety Disorder
	300.21	Panic Disorder with Agoraphobia
	300.01	Panic Disorder without Agoraphobia
	300.23	Social Phobia
	300.29	Specific Phobia
	_____	_____
	_____	_____
Axis II:	301.82	Avoidant Personality Disorder
	301.83	Borderline Personality Disorder
	301.50	Histrionic Personality Disorder
	_____	_____
	_____	_____

POSTTRAUMATIC STRESS DISORDER (PTSD)

BEHAVIORAL DEFINITIONS

1. Exposure to a life event that is outside the range of usual human experiences, that involved actual or threatened death or serious injury.
2. Witness to or involvement in a traumatic event that threatened the physical integrity of self or others.
3. Subjective experience of intense fear, helplessness, or horror.
4. Recurrent, intrusive, traumatic memories, nightmares, and/or hallucinations related to an event.
5. Acting or feeling as if the traumatic event were recurring through illusions; emotionally reliving the experience or dissociative flashback experiences.
6. Intense psychological distress during exposure to events, places, or people that are reminders of the traumatic event.
7. Persistent avoidance of stimuli associated with the traumatic event.
8. Inability to recall important aspects of the traumatic event.
9. Exaggerated startle response or hypervigilance.
10. Easily enraged, frequent outbursts of anger.
11. Difficulty concentrating, anhedonia, detachment or estrangement from others.
12. Sense of foreshortened future.

—. _____

—. _____

—. _____

LONG-TERM GOALS

1. Report the termination of intrusive memories, nightmares, flash-backs, and hallucinations.
2. Assimilate the traumatic event into life and place it into perspective.
3. Return to the level of occupational, psychological, and social functioning present before the traumatic event.
4. Remember the traumatic event accurately without debilitating emotional responses.
5. Feel empowered in daily functioning with a restored sense of dignity and increased feeling of personal security.
6. Regain self-confidence, emotional control, sociability, and a sense of serenity and joy.

—. _____
_____
—. _____
_____
—. _____
_____

SHORT-TERM OBJECTIVES

1. Provide a complete biopsychosocial history. (1, 2)
2. Identify any substance abuse, and maintain sobriety during treatment. (3, 4, 5)
3. Cooperate with psychosocial testing to assess PTSD symptom pattern. (6)
4. Identify any secondary gain attained from PTSD symptoms. (6, 7)
5. Identify and obtain treatment for any medical problems that may contribute to

THERAPEUTIC INTERVENTIONS

1. Establish a rapport with the client by providing reassurance and warmth. Explain the necessity of obtaining a psychosocial history, and tell the client that he/she is in control of what information is provided.
2. Conduct a comprehensive psychosocial assessment including pretrauma functioning, the nature of the trauma, response of social support at the time of the trauma, and the impact of

impairment or inhibit psychological treatment. (8)

6. Comply with an evaluation for psychotropic medication. (9)

7. Participate in specialized inpatient treatment for PTSD. (10)

8. Identify people who can be relied upon for social support. (11, 12)

9. Family and/or friends verbalize an increased understanding of ways to assist the client's recovery. (13, 14, 15)

10. Write a plan to engage other people for emotional support. (16)

11. Attend a support group for people suffering the consequences of traumatic experiences. (17)

12. List the ways in which the traumatic event has impacted life. (2, 18, 19)

13. Verbalize a decrease in anger and ways to effectively manage anger. (20, 21, 22, 23, 24)

14. Clarify memories of the traumatic event(s). (25, 26, 27)

15. Report flashbacks or dissociative experiences. (27, 28, 29)

16. Verbalize feelings of survival guilt. (30, 31)

17. Verbalize an understanding of the use of Subjective

the trauma upon psychosocial functioning.

3. Assess the client for any drug and/or alcohol abuse; if chemical dependence is present, refrain from treating the PTSD until abstinence has been achieved.

4. Refer the client to a substance abuse program for random drug testing.

5. Refer the client to a substance abuse treatment program and/or a 12-step group to help him/her establish and maintain sobriety.

6. Conduct psychological testing (e.g., Minnesota Multiphasic Personality Inventory, PTSD Symptom Scale, Impact of Events Scale, etc.) to determine the nature and severity of the impairment and rule out malingering.

7. Inquire about possible secondary gain reasons that the client might want to obtain a diagnosis of PTSD, such as gaining Veteran's disability benefits, workers' compensation, and so on.

8. Refer the client to a medical doctor for a comprehensive examination for any problems (e.g., neurological impairments, heart conditions, etc.) that may contribute to impairment or inhibit further psychological treatment.

Units of Distress (SUDs).
(32)

18. Cooperate with flooding
procedures that require recalling details of the traumatic event. (33)

19. Listen to audiotapes of the
description of the traumatic
event(s) between sessions.
(34)

20. Cooperate with an eye
movement desensitization
and reprocessing (EMDR)
technique to reduce emo-
tional reaction to the traumatic event. (35)

21. Practice relaxation techniques. (36)

22. Practice systematic desensitization through imaginal
exposure to the traumatic
event. (37)

23. Practice thought-stopping
techniques to decrease and
replace intrusive thoughts
and ruminations. (38)

24. Challenge cognitive distortions that are related to the
traumatic event, and re-
place them with more realistic beliefs. (39, 40)

25. List five ways to prevent
posttraumatic stress reactions. (41)

26. Write a coping skills plan
that details what to do
when experiencing symp-
toms. (42)

27. Participate in a ritual that
assists with putting the
traumatic event in the past.
(43)

9. Refer the client to a physician for a psychotropic medication evaluation, and
monitor his/her compliance
with the physician's orders.

10. Assist the client with locating specialized inpatient
PTSD treatment, and ar-
range for him/her to be ad-
mitted if the symptoms
cause a serious debilitation
in functioning.

11. Inquire as to the nature of
the client's social support
system, and encourage
him/her to utilize this resource during treatment.

12. Have the client draw an eco-
map to graphically depict
available social support.
Probe the client regarding a
full range of possibilities, including friends, family, religious leaders, coworkers,
neighbors, classmates, and
others.

13. Conduct a family therapy
session in which the client
and his/her family share
feelings and offer emotional
support, understanding,
and comfort.

14. Assess whether there are
marital or family conflicts
that are the result of PTSD.

15. Educate the family regarding how they may be en-
abling the client to avoid
confronting and resolving
his/her PTSD issues (e.g.,
supporting the client's use
of substances, avoidance,
denial, etc.).

28. List coping techniques that will be implemented at times of high risk of symptom relapse. (44)

—. _____
_____

—. _____
_____

—. _____
_____

16. Assign the client homework of writing an action plan to increase emotional support from others that may include time spent with supportive people. Monitor progress with implementing plan.

17. Assist the client in locating support groups for people who are suffering from similar traumatic events (e.g., Veteran's support groups, adults molested as children, etc.), and encourage him/her to attend in order to decrease social isolation.

18. Ask the client to make a list of the ways in which the traumatic event has impacted his/her life and to process the list with a therapist.

19. Monitor the client for distress in moods such as depression or anxiety. (See the chapters entitled "Depression" or "Anxiety" in this planner).

20. Gently confront the client regarding any misdirected anger. Remind him/her of the stages of grieving in which anger is a common component.

21. Interpret anger as a symptom of feeling helpless. Process the reactions to the interpretations in session.

22. Teach the client to release anger physically by hitting a punching bag or pillows; process all such releases.

23. Utilize the therapeutic game Stop, Relax, and Think (Shapiro) to assist the client in developing self-control.

24. Recommend that the client read *Of Course You're Angry* (Rosellini and Worden), *The Angry Book* (Rubin), or *The Anger Workout Book* (Weisinger).

25. Facilitate the client's recall of the details of the traumatic event(s) by asking him/her to journal, talk about, and think about the incident(s). Caution the client against embellishment based on book, video, or drama material, and do not lead the client into only confirming therapist-held suspicions.

26. Encourage the client to obtain accurate corroboration of the traumatic event through contacting witnesses (other veterans, siblings, bystanders, etc.) and any written materials (medical reports, newspaper articles, police reports, etc.).

27. Ask the client to recall sights, sounds, smells, and tactile feelings during the event. Identify how a flashback can occur when these senses are triggered by an unexpected exposure during routine, daily functioning.

28. Educate the client regarding flashbacks and/or dissociative experiences and how they are often transitory

and triggered by daily events or thoughts of the traumatic event.

29. Utilizing self-talk techniques, teach the client to process through a flashback by focusing on the facts and internally validating the fear that he/she feels.

30. Ask the client to share his/her role in the event; focus on his/her feelings of helplessness and placing blame on the perpetrator versus himself/herself.

31. When the client expresses guilt/self-blame, redirect him/her to view the event as something that happened beyond his/her control, placing the blame on the perpetrator or event.

32. Educate the client on the use of Subjective Units of Distress (SUDs). Ask him/her to rank each traumatic memory on a scale of 1 to 10, with 10 being the most distressing.

33. Have the client describe in graphic detail (using sounds, sights, smells, emotions, etc.) the memories of the traumatic event, beginning with less anxiety-provoking memories to assist with desensitization.

34. Assign the client homework of listening to her/his tape-recorded description of the event/assault to increase desensitization to the traumatic event(s).

35. Conduct eye movement desensitization and reprocessing (EMDR).

36. Teach the client relaxation techniques: deep-breathing exercises, progressive muscle relaxation, cue-controlled relaxation, and/or differential relaxation.

37. Have the client induce relaxation and then recall aspects of the traumatic event that gradually increase in anxiety induction. Continue until the client reports that the image is less anxiety provoking.

38. Educate the client regarding thought-stopping techniques, including saying no when intrusive thoughts are present, snapping a rubber band on the wrist, and replacing negative thoughts with more pleasant thoughts.

39. Teach the client how to use an automatic thought record to identify distorted cognitions related to the traumatic event.

40. Use cognitive restructuring techniques to replace distorted cognitions with more realistic positive thoughts.

41. Teach the client ways to prevent PTSD reactions (e.g., maintaining healthy eating, getting ample rest, participation in leisure activities, avoiding substance use, and setting realistic goals for the future).

42. Review with the client the methods that have worked best to decrease distress and assign him/her homework of writing a plan to use these methods (e.g., utilizing social support, thought stopping, relaxation techniques, etc.) when experiencing symptoms.

43. Encourage the client to participate in a ritual that assists him/her with placing the traumatic event in the past (e.g., visiting the Vietnam Veteran's Memorial Wall, the Holocaust Museum, etc.).

44. Prompt the client to talk about how the pain or alteration of his/her life that has resulted from the traumatic event has increased with the approaching anniversary of the event or other trigger events (i.e., court proceedings, vicarious exposure through media, etc.); develop alternative coping techniques for these trigger events.

___.   _____
       _____

___.   _____
       _____

___.   _____
       _____

DIAGNOSTIC SUGGESTIONS

Axis I: 308.3   Acute Stress Disorder

                    309.xx   Adjustment Disorder

                    303.90   Alcohol Dependence

                    296.xx   Bipolar I Disorder

                    300.6   Depersonalization Disorder

                    300.12   Dissociative Amnesia

                    300.14   Dissociative Identity Disorder

                    300.4   Dysthymic Disorder

                    300.02   Generalized Anxiety Disorder

                    296.xx   Major Depressive Disorder

                    V65.2   Malingering

                    304.80   Polysubstance Dependence

                    309.81   Posttraumatic Stress Disorder

                    295.70   Schizoaffective Disorder

_____   _____

_____   _____

Axis II: 301.7   Antisocial Personality Disorder

                    301.82   Avoidant Personality Disorder

                    301.83   Borderline Personality Disorder

                    301.50   Histrionic Personality Disorder

                    301.9   Personality Disorder NOS

_____   _____

_____   _____

SCHOOL TRAUMA (PREELEMENTARY)

BEHAVIORAL DEFINITIONS

1. The traumatic, sudden death or serious injury of a student or faculty member (e.g., due to SIDS, choking, accident, playground incident, school bus tragedy, natural disaster, bomb explosion, etc.).
2. Death of a student or faculty member who had a terminal illness.
3. Stalking or child kidnapping in the vicinity of the preschool and/or child care facility.
4. An outsider who is in the building, threatening violence to anyone.
5. Dramatic damage to the building caused by fire, bomb threat, chemical infiltration through the heating/cooling system, or a natural disaster (tornado, earthquake, flood).
6. Persistent reluctance to be separated from parents.
7. Difficulty with sleep and/or nightmares about the traumatic event.
8. Physical complaints of headaches, stomach aches, loss of bladder and/or bowel control or other regressive behaviors since the traumatic incident.
9. Grief expressed in sadness, tearfulness, and/or withdrawal.

—. _____

—. _____

—. _____

LONG-TERM GOALS

1. Return to pretrauma level of functioning.
2. Reduce the risk of long-term psychological distress.

3. Receive the psychological and social support necessary to adapt to the traumatic event.
4. Grieve and cope with the loss in a healthy, appropriate manner.

—. _____
_____
_____

—. _____
_____
_____

—. _____
_____

SHORT-TERM OBJECTIVES

1. Staff, family members, and law enforcement officials provide actual/factual information about the traumatic event. (1)
2. Staff identify any missing children. (2)
3. Staff account for and monitor the location of the children at all times. (3, 4)
4. Children and their parents gather together. (5, 6)
5. Staff identify children who are at high risk for a severe emotional reaction to the trauma. (7, 8)
6. Children needing immediate mental health professional attention access such services. (9, 10)
7. Children with their parents listen to the facts of the traumatic incident. (6, 11, 12)

THERAPEUTIC INTERVENTIONS

1. Communicate openly with school staff, law enforcement, medical personnel, or the deceased's family to determine the details or suspected cause of the traumatic event.
2. Ask the staff to retrieve the daily attendance sheet indicating the children who are present/missing.
3. Educate the staff on the importance of monitoring the location of the children at all times. Encourage them to use a daily attendance sheet to keep track of the movement of the children, noting time left and time returned.
4. Designate a facility administrator to operate a sign-in/ message center. Have all individuals (parents, staff, crisis response team members, community support members, etc.) entering and

8. Children express their emotional reactions to the event. (13, 14, 15)

9. Children verbalize an understanding of the fact that the deceased child will not return. (16, 17)

10. Children verbalize a decreased belief in negative magical thinking associated with the trauma. (17, 18, 19)

11. Children verbalize a realistic understanding of the cause of the trauma and indicate that blame does not rest with themselves. (19, 20, 21)

12. Children verbalize feeling safe and that the danger is over. (6, 18, 22, 23, 24)

13. Children demonstrate a decrease in fear of being alone. (24, 25, 26)

14. Children verbalize their nightmares and coping strategies for them. (27, 28)

15. Children differentiate between imaginary and real friends. (29, 30)

16. Children demonstrate a decrease in regressive behaviors such as thumb sucking, clinging, enuresis, or encopresis. (31)

17. Children identify people with whom they can comfortably share their feelings. (32, 33)

18. Facility personnel write a plan to disseminate infor-

leaving the school register on a sign-in/out log.

5. Make immediate contact with the parents/guardians, and have them come to the facility quickly.

6. Encourage the parents/guardians to stay at the facility with their child for a brief amount of time so they can be informed about the event and so the child does not see the facility as a place of ongoing danger.

7. Educate the school staff about the high-risk reaction criteria such as any children who: are close friends or relatives of the victim(s); have a history of mental illness; have already experienced a significant loss; were absent the day following the initial response; have inadequate support systems; witnessed the trauma; self-identify as at risk.

8. Utilize psychological tests to assess the mental status of the children [i.e., the Reynolds Child Depression Scale or the Trauma Symptom Checklist for Children (Briere)].

9. Assess each child's level of emotional distress to identify those who appear to be a high risk for complications in their reaction and need immediate intervention and/or referral for intensive mental health attention.

mation to the children, parents, and the community. (34, 35)

19. Facility personnel provide accurate and appropriate information to parents, children, and the community according to a written plan. (35, 36)

20. Parents express their thoughts and feelings about the tragedy. (37)

21. Parents verbalize an increased understanding of the signs and symptoms of acute and delayed stress reactions. (38, 39)

22. Children utilize coping strategies taught to help them cope with the traumatic event. (40)

23. Facility personnel participate in a critical incident stress debriefing and/or daily debriefings. (41, 42, 43)

24. Facility staff return to structured, routine operating schedule. (44, 45)

25. Parents advise school staff of any significant behavioral changes in the children. (45, 46)

26. Teachers/caretakers or parents identify any delayed symptoms of distress. (38, 39, 47)

27. Children discuss the future in positive terms. (48)

28. Staff develop a written plan to address the ongoing

10. Refer high-risk reactive children to the appropriate mental health professional(s) within the school system as well as in the community; facilitate the follow-through on this referral through contact with the family and the mental health professional.

11. Inform the children and their parents in a joint meeting of the facts that are associated with the traumatic event. Encourage the children's expression of thoughts and feelings about the event. Normalize feelings of sadness, anger, fear, frustration, and grief.

12. Separate the facts of what happened from the fantasy of what the children may be recalling. Describe the events as very, very, very rare.

13. Utilize play therapy techniques (coloring books, building blocks, and dolls or puppets) to help the children express their emotions. Help the children put their feelings and ideas into words by providing emotional labels for common reactions demonstrated in the play therapy.

14. Encourage the children to watch videos regarding a trauma or stress reaction (e.g., *Winnie the Pooh: The Blustery Day; Veggie Tales: Where's God When I Am*

needs of the children, parents, and staff. (49)

—. _____
_____

—. _____
_____

—. _____
_____

Scared, or similar movies). Discuss with the children how those characters cope with loss and express their grief.

15. Encourage play reenactment of the student's experience and observations during the traumatic event. Permit the child to act out his/her memories, correcting distortions, and acknowledging the normalcy of the reactions.

16. Discuss the issue of death openly and concretely using the words *dead* and *died.* Inform the children that death is permanent, and the deceased child will not return to the facility.

17. Provide explanations about the physical reality of death to the children. Avoid use of euphemistic terminology that denies the reality of death (e.g., stating the deceased child is forever sleeping).

18. In discussions with the children, separate what happened as being different from physical reminders (e.g., the place where the incident occurred).

19. Assess the children's egocentricity and magical thinking regarding the deaths. Use puppets to explore if they are wondering if their actions may have caused the death.

20. Reassure the children that they are not to blame for the deaths of the children or faculty; explain the realistic cause in an open and direct fashion without increasing the students' fear.

21. Encourage the staff to offer educational presentations from doctors, police, or the American Red Cross regarding first aid, choking, rescue work, and so on.

22. Encourage the children to touch the physical structure of the facility, hit it with hammers, inspect it carefully, and so on to reinforce their sense of safety.

23. Role-play situations that promote the child's feelings of safety (e.g., call 911, sound the fire alarm or door exit alarm, ask to see parent's identification when picking up the children, etc.). Observe their reactions to the emergency notification sounds, and offer comfort and compassion if they appear bothered.

24. Reestablish the child's perception of an adult protective shield by increasing the parents' involvement at the facility and providing reassurance that the child will be picked up by a parent/guardian.

25. Encourage the staff to make clocks stating the time when each child's parent is

to pick the child up. Compare the crafted clock with a real clock to decrease the child's anxiety about being picked up.

26. Increase the number of adults present at the facility, keeping close proximity to the children at all times to decrease the children's fear of being left alone.

27. Ask the children to report if they are having nightmares or bad dreams. Discuss emotional reactions to dreams in session.

28. Teach the children how to cope with nightmares by talking to their parents, opening their eyes, holding onto a favorite toy or blanket, and so forth.

29. Explore the onset of the child developing imaginary friends. Encourage the child to express himself/herself through the imaginary friend.

30. Separate reality from fantasy for the child. Take note if an imaginary friend bears the same name, gender, or characteristics of the deceased child, and encourage the child's expression of grief at missing the deceased acquaintance.

31. Monitor the student's regressive behaviors and attitudes; affirm the normalcy of regression while encouraging age-appropriate re-

sponses. Refer the student for individual counseling if symptoms persist.

32. Use a genogram to identify people with whom the children feel comfortable sharing their feelings (e.g., family members, teachers, counselors, adult neighbors, religious leaders, etc.).

33. Encourage the children to talk with their parents about the traumatic experience and their feelings surrounding the experience.

34. Assist facility personnel in writing a plan for communicating information about the tragedy to parents, the children, and the community; facilitate policy implementation.

35. Advise the staff to refer to the facility's crisis response plan manual for guidelines in writing memos, statements, handouts, media releases, and so on.

36. Review all informational material to ensure that it is consistent with other information being disseminated.

37. Conduct evening groups for parents in which they are given the opportunity to discuss their concerns, express their emotional reactions about the trauma, and are provided information about acute and delayed stress reactions in children.

38. Teach the parents the benefits of asking their children daily about their activities of the day and their thoughts experienced throughout the day.

39. Send educational handouts, describing the symptoms of delayed stress reactions, home with the children one month after the incident.

40. Teach the children the benefits of painting/coloring, using drama to act out their feelings, using dolls/stuffed animals to communicate how they feel, or telling their parents about the need for being close to them.

41. Facilitate a critical incident stress debriefing for the facility staff to decrease their distress over the event and increase their ability to provide support to the children.

42. Allow time each day for the facility staff to debrief, to express their emotions, and to verbalize how this situation has had an impact on them.

43. Sensitize the staff as to how they have been affected by the traumatic event, and redirect the staff when they focus solely on the students' needs.

44. Encourage the staff to return to a normal operating schedule, allowing enough flexibility to be responsive to any children needing to talk about the event.

45. Address the need for increased structured play time and rest time as the children assimilate the trauma into their lives. Teach the need for increased awareness of behavioral reactions likely to occur during these times, and to reinforce good communication with the children's parents regarding what is being observed.

46. Encourage parents to communicate to teachers/caretakers any concerns about what they are seeing at home (and vice versa) in terms of the child's trauma reaction.

47. Utilize the Trauma Symptom Checklist for Children (Briere) on a weekly basis to assess children's delayed reactions to the event.

48. Reaffirm the future to the children and the staff. Talk in hopeful terms. Mention positive plans and rebuilding; reinforce any future talk by the children and staff.

49. Assist school staff in writing a plan to address the ongoing needs of the children, parents, and staff, specifying actions to be taken over the next year such as the distribution of mailings, monitoring for symptoms of delayed stress, referring to appropriate supportive services, and

preparing for anniversary
reactions.

—. _____
_____

—. _____
_____

—. _____
_____

DIAGNOSTIC SUGGESTIONS

Axis I:	V62.3	Academic Problems
	308.3	Acute Stress Disorder
	309.xx	Adjustment Disorder
	V62.82	Bereavement
	300.14	Dissociative Identity Disorder
	307.7	Encopresis
	307.6	Enuresis
	307.47	Nightmare Disorder
	309.81	Posttraumatic Stress Disorder
	309.21	Separation Anxiety Disorder
	_____	_____
	_____	_____
Axis II:	V71.09	No Diagnosis
	_____	_____
	_____	_____

SCHOOL TRAUMA (ELEMENTARY)

BEHAVIORAL DEFINITIONS

1. The traumatic, sudden death or serious injury of student(s) or faculty member(s) (e.g., due to suicide, accident, homicide, playground incident, school bus tragedy, natural disaster, bomb explosion, etc.).
2. Death of a student or faculty member who had a prolonged illness.
3. Stalking or child kidnapping in the vicinity of the school.
4. An outsider who is in the building, threatening violence to anyone.
5. Dramatic school damage caused by fire, bomb threat, boiler blowup, chemical infiltration through the heating/cooling system, or a natural disaster (tornado, earthquake, flood).
6. Persistent reluctance to leave the house to attend school and be separated from parents.
7. Difficulty with sleep and/or nightmares about the traumatic event.
8. Physical complaints of headaches, nausea, loss of bladder and/or bowel control, or other regressive behaviors since the traumatic incident.
9. Preoccupation with death and/or an increased verbalization of suicidal thoughts.
10. Grief expressed in sadness, tearfulness, and/or withdrawal.

—. _____
   _____

—. _____
   _____

—. _____
   _____

LONG-TERM GOALS

1. Return to pretrauma level of functioning.
2. Reduce the risk of long-term psychological distress.
3. Receive the psychological and social support necessary to adapt to the traumatic event.
4. Grieve and cope with the loss in a healthy, appropriate manner.
5. Overcome the fear of harm, and return to a normal level of functioning.

—. _____
   _____
—. _____
   _____
—. _____
   _____

SHORT-TERM OBJECTIVES

1. Staff, students, family members, and law enforcement officials provide actual/factual information about the traumatic event. (1)

2. School staff identify any missing students. (2)

3. School staff account for and monitor the location of the students at all times. (3, 4)

4. School personnel identify students who are at high risk for a severe emotional reaction to the trauma. (5, 6, 8)

5. Selected high-risk students participate in individual crisis intervention to get support. (7, 8)

THERAPEUTIC INTERVENTIONS

1. Communicate openly with school staff, law enforcement, medical personnel, or the deceased's family to determine the details or suspected cause of the traumatic event.

2. Ask the school staff to retrieve the daily attendance sheet of each classroom indicating the students who are present/missing.

3. Educate the school staff on the importance of monitoring the location of the students at all times. Encourage them to use a daily attendance sheet to keep track of the movement of the students, noting time left and time returned.

6. Students needing immediate mental health professional attention access such services. (8, 9)

7. Students verbalize an understanding of the facts of the traumatic incident and reject false information. (10, 11, 14)

8. Students express their emotional reactions to the event. (6, 12, 13, 14)

9. Students verbalize an increased understanding of the concept of death. (15, 16)

10. Students verbalize a realistic understanding of the cause of the trauma and indicate that blame does not rest with themselves. (16, 17)

11. Students verbalize their nightmares and coping strategies for them. (18, 19)

12. Students demonstrate a decrease in regressive behaviors such as thumb sucking, clinging, enuresis, or encopresis. (20)

13. Students identify people with whom they can comfortably share their feelings. (21, 22, 23)

14. Students increase communication with parents and teachers. (22, 23)

15. School personnel write a plan to disseminate information to the students, parents, and the community. (24)

4. Designate a school official to operate a sign-in/message center. Have all individuals (students, staff, crisis response team members, community support members, etc.) entering and leaving the school register on a sign-in/out log.

5. Educate the school staff about the high-risk reaction criteria such as any students who: are close friends or relatives of the victim(s), have a history of mental illness, have already experienced a significant loss, were absent the day following the initial response, have inadequate support systems, witnessed the trauma, self-identify as at risk.

6. Utilize psychological tests to assess the mental status of the students [i.e., the Reynolds Child Depression Scale, the Symptom Checklist 90, or the Trauma Symptom Checklist for Children (Briere)].

7. Establish rapport with and give support to the high-risk student in an individual session by providing reassurance and warmth, maintaining eye contact, and speaking with a calm and confident voice while the student talks about his/her feelings associated with the trauma.

8. Assess each student's level of emotional distress to

16. School personnel provide accurate and appropriate information to parents, students, and the community according to a written plan. (24, 25, 26)

17. Parents express their thoughts and feelings about the tragedy. (27)

18. Parents verbalize an increased understanding of the signs and symptoms of delayed stress reactions. (27, 28, 29)

19. Students utilize coping strategies taught to help them cope with the traumatic event. (30)

20. School personnel participate in a critical incident stress debriefing and/or daily debriefings. (31, 32, 33)

21. Students say good-bye to the deceased student. (34)

22. School staff return to normal operating schedule. (35)

23. Parents advise school staff of any significant behavioral changes in the students. (36)

24. Teachers or parents identify any delayed symptoms of distress. (27, 29, 36, 37)

25. Students discuss the future in positive terms. (38)

26. Students and staff attend and participate in a memorial to the deceased. (39, 40)

27. School staff develop a written plan to address the on-

identify those who appear to be a high risk for complications in their reactions and need immediate intervention and/or referral for intensive mental health attention.

9. Refer high-risk students to the appropriate mental health professional(s) within the school system as well as in the community; facilitate the follow-through on this referral through contact with the family and the mental health professional.

10. Ask the students to describe the facts associated with the traumatic event and the thoughts that they have about it. Normalize feelings of sadness, anger, fear, frustration, and grief, keeping the debriefing to less than an hour to prevent students from being overwhelmed.

11. Separate the facts of what happened from the fantasy of what the students may be recalling. Describe the events as very, very, very rare.

12. Utilize play therapy techniques by using coloring books and dolls or puppets. Ask the students to describe their emotional reactions through the use of these props.

13. Encourage the students to draw what they are afraid of as well as drawing good

going needs of the students, parents, and staff. (41)

__. _____
      _____

__. _____
      _____

__. _____
      _____

things (i.e., rescue workers coming to help, pictures of sun and trees, etc.).

14. Encourage play reenactment of the student's experience and observations during the traumatic event. Permit the child to act out his/her memories, correcting distortions, and acknowledging the normalcy of the reactions.

15. Discuss the issue of death openly and concretely using the words *dead* and *died*. Inform the students that death is permanent. Process emotional reactions in session, and answer any questions directly.

16. Assess the students' egocentricity and magical thinking regarding the deaths. Use puppets to explore if they are wondering if their actions may have caused the death.

17. Reassure the students that they are not to blame for the deaths of the students or faculty; explain the realistic cause in an open and direct fashion without increasing the students' fear.

18. Ask the students to report if they are having nightmares or bad dreams. Discuss emotional reactions to dreams in session.

19. Teach the students how to cope with nightmares by talking to their parents,

opening their eyes, holding onto a favorite toy or blanket, and so forth.

20. Monitor the student's regressive behaviors and attitudes; affirm the normalcy of regression while encouraging age-appropriate responses. Refer the student for individual counseling if symptoms persist.

21. Use a genogram to identify people with whom the students feel comfortable sharing their feelings (e.g., family members, teachers, counselors, adult neighbors, religious leaders, etc.).

22. Encourage the students to talk with their parents about the traumatic experience and their feelings surrounding the experience.

23. Encourage the students to share with their teachers when their thoughts and feelings about the trauma are interfering with their learning.

24. Assist school personnel in writing a plan for communicating information about the tragedy to parents, the students, and the community; facilitate policy implementation.

25. Advise the staff to refer to the school's crisis response plan manual for guidelines in writing memos, statements, handouts, media releases, and so on.

26. Review all informational material to ensure that it is consistent with other information being disseminated.

27. Conduct evening groups for parents in which they are given the opportunity to discuss their concerns, express their emotional reactions about the trauma, and are provided information about acute and delayed stress reactions in the students.

28. Teach the parents the benefits of asking their children daily about their activities of the day and their thoughts experienced throughout the day.

29. Send home with the students one month following the incident, educational handouts describing the symptoms of acute and delayed stress reactions.

30. Teach the students the benefits of drawing/coloring, using drama to act out their feelings, using dolls/stuffed animals to communicate how they feel, or telling their parents about the need for hugs or time alone.

31. Facilitate a critical incident stress debriefing for the school staff to decrease their distress over the event and increase their ability to provide support to the students.

32. Allow time each day for the school staff to debrief, to ex-

press their emotions, and to verbalize how this situation has had an impact on them.

33. Sensitize the staff as to how they have been affected by the traumatic event, and redirect the staff when they focus solely on the students' needs.

34. Conduct a session in which the students say good-bye to the deceased friend using the empty-chair (Perls) technique to allow the students to talk to the deceased child. Remove the chair from the classroom. Process emotional reactions to the exercise.

35. Encourage the staff to return to a normal operating schedule, allowing enough flexibility to be responsive to any students needing to talk about the event.

36. Encourage parents to communicate to teachers any concerns about what they are seeing at home (and vice versa) in terms of the child's trauma reaction.

37. Utilize the Trauma Symptom Checklist for Children (Briere) on a weekly basis to assess students' delayed reactions to the event.

38. Reaffirm the future to the students and the staff. Talk in hopeful terms. Mention positive plans and rebuilding; reinforce any future talk by the students and staff.

39. Assist in planning a memorial commemoration in honor of the deceased in which the staff and students may take part.

40. Encourage the students and staff to memorialize the deceased with their own expressions of remembrance (e.g., a poem, drawing, flower, photo, etc.); designate a place for collection of such remembrances.

41. Assist school staff in writing a plan to address the ongoing needs of the students, parents, and staff, specifying actions to be taken over the next year such as the distribution of mailings, monitoring for symptoms of delayed stress, referring to appropriate supportive services, and preparing for anniversary reactions.

__. _____

_____

__. _____

_____

__. _____

_____

DIAGNOSTIC SUGGESTIONS

Axis I: V62.3   Academic Problems
308.3   Acute Stress Disorder
309.xx   Adjustment Disorder
V62.82   Bereavement
307.7   Encopresis

	307.6	Enuresis
	307.47	Nightmare Disorder
	313.81	Oppositional Defiant Disorder
	309.81	Posttraumatic Stress Disorder
	309.21	Separation Anxiety Disorder
	_____	_____
	_____	_____
Axis II:	V71.09	No Diagnosis
	_____	_____
	_____	_____

SCHOOL TRAUMA (SECONDARY)

BEHAVIORAL DEFINITIONS

1. The traumatic, sudden death or serious injury of student(s) or faculty member(s) (e.g., due to suicide, motor vehicle accident, homicide, school bus tragedy, natural disaster, bomb explosion, etc.).
2. Death of a student or faculty member who had a prolonged illness.
3. Sudden death of a student while participating in an athletic or extracurricular activity.
4. Stalking or child kidnapping in the vicinity of the school.
5. An outsider who is in the building, threatening violence to anyone.
6. Dramatic school damage caused by fire, bomb explosion or bomb threat, boiler blowup, chemical infiltration through the heating/cooling system, or a natural disaster (tornado, earthquake, flood).
7. Persistent reluctance to leave the house to attend school and becoming withdrawn.
8. Difficulty with sleep and/or nightmares about the traumatic event.
9. Physical complaints of headaches, nausea, loss of breath, gastrointestinal problems, loss of appetite, or overeating.
10. Preoccupation with death and/or an increased verbalization of suicidal thoughts.
11. Feelings of irrational guilt regarding having been a survivor of the trauma while others died.
12. Persistent fear of death or personal injury occurring to self.
13. Grief expressed in sadness, tearfulness, and/or isolating self from peers/family.

__. _____
    _____

__. _____
    _____

—. _____
  _____

LONG-TERM GOALS

1. Return to pretrauma level of functioning.
2. Reduce the risk of long-term psychological distress.
3. Receive the psychological and social support necessary to adapt to the traumatic event.
4. Grieve and develop healthy coping mechanisms following the traumatic event.
5. Overcome fear of harm, and return to a normal level of functioning.
6. Relieve irrational guilt, and accept the reality of the loss and its real cause.

—. _____
  _____
—. _____
  _____
—. _____
  _____

SHORT-TERM OBJECTIVES

1. Staff, students, family members, and law enforcement officials provide factual information about the traumatic event. (1)

2. School staff identify any missing students. (2)

3. School staff account for and monitor the location of students at all times. (3, 4)

4. School personnel identify students who are at high risk for a severe emotional

THERAPEUTIC INTERVENTIONS

1. Communicate openly with school staff, law enforcement, medical personnel, or the deceased's family to determine the details and suspected cause of the traumatic event.

2. Ask the school staff to retrieve the daily attendance sheet of each home room/grade, indicating students who are present/missing.

3. Educate the school staff on the importance of monitor-

reaction to the trauma. (5, 6, 8)

5. Selected high-risk students participate in individual crisis intervention to get support. (7, 8)

6. Students needing immediate mental health professional attention access such services. (8, 9)

7. Students describe the facts of the traumatic incident accurately and reject false information. (10, 11)

8. Students express their emotional reactions to the event. (8, 10, 12)

9. Students identify feelings of aggression and anger. (12, 13)

10. Students remain active and not withdrawn or isolating themselves. (14)

11. Students verbalize an increased understanding of the concept of death. (15, 16)

12. Students verbalize a realistic understanding of the cause of the trauma and indicate that blame does not rest with themselves. (17)

13. Students identify any use of alcohol or other substances as a means of coping with the traumatic event. (18, 19)

14. Students verbalize any thoughts of suicide. (20)

15. Students identify trusted people with whom they can share their feelings about this incident. (21, 22, 23)

ing the location of students at all times. Encourage them to use an attendance sheet to keep track of the movement of students, noting time left and time returned.

4. Designate a school official to operate a sign-in/message center. Have all individuals (students, staff, crisis response team members, community support members, etc.) entering and leaving the school register on a sign-in/out log.

5. Educate the school staff about the high-risk reaction criteria such as any students who: are close friends or relatives of the victim; have a history of mental illness, have active suicidal ideation or demonstrate suicidal behaviors, have already experienced a significant loss, were absent the day following the initial response, have inadequate or a damaged support system, witnessed the trauma, self-identify as at risk.

6. Utilize psychological tests to assess the mental status of students [i.e., the Reynolds Child Depression Scale, the Symptom Checklist 90, or the Trauma Symptom Checklist for Adolescents (Briere)].

7. Establish rapport with the student by providing reassurance and warmth, main-

16. Students increase communication with parents and teachers. (22, 23, 30)

17. School personnel write a plan to disseminate information to the students, parents, and community. (24)

18. School personnel provide accurate and appropriate information to parents, students, and the community according to a written plan. (24, 25, 26)

19. Parents express their thoughts and feelings about the tragedy. (27)

20. Parents verbalize an increased understanding of the signs and symptoms of acute and delayed stress reactions. (27, 28, 29)

21. Students utilize coping strategies taught to help them cope with the traumatic event. (30)

22. School personnel participate in a critical incident stress debriefing and/or daily debriefings. (31, 32, 33)

23. Students say good-bye to their deceased peer. (34, 35)

24. School staff return to a normal operating schedule. (36)

25. Parents advise school staff of any significant behavioral changes in their children. (37)

26. Teachers or parents identify any delayed symptoms of distress. (27, 29, 37, 38)

taining eye contact, and speaking with a calm and confident voice as support is given in an individual crisis intervention.

8. Assess each student's level of emotional distress to identify those who appear to be a high risk for complications in their reactions and need immediate intervention and/or referral for intensive mental health attention.

9. Refer high-risk students to the appropriate mental health professional(s) within the school system as well as in the community; facilitate the follow-through on this referral through contact with the family and the mental health professional.

10. Ask the students to describe the facts associated with the event and the feelings that they have about it. Normalize feelings of fear, anger, frustration, and grief.

11. Separate the facts of what happened from the false rumors that the students may be hearing.

12. Address the realistic consequences of students' revengeful, aggressive actions. Encourage constructive expressions of anger through exercise, use of punching bags, and so forth.

27. Students discuss the future in positive terms. (39)

28. Students and staff attend and participate in a memorial to the deceased. (35, 40, 41)

29. School staff develop a written plan to address the ongoing needs of the students, parents, and staff. (42)

__. _____
_____

__. _____
_____

__. _____
_____

13. Complete a homicide assessment on students who are enraged overtly or covertly. Make contact with individuals who may be at risk of harm.

14. Ask the students to keep an activity log, documenting their time spent alone, on the computer, sleeping, playing video games, socializing, and so forth.

15. Discuss the issue of death openly and concretely using the words *dead* and *died*. Assess the students' egocentricity and magical thinking regarding the deaths.

16. Ask the student to share past experiences regarding death of a loved one or a pet. Identify coping mechanisms used to manage grief in a healthy, constructive way.

17. Reassure the students that they are not to blame for the deaths of the students or faculty; redirect the students to place the blame on the perpetrator.

18. Assess the students for any pattern of alcohol and/or drug abuse. If present, refer him/her to a substance abuse treatment program.

19. Teach the students how using substances to escape or feel numb produces further complications and problems. Offer alternative coping mechanisms of jour-

naling, exercising, meditation, sharing feelings, and so forth.

20. Conduct a suicide assessment, noting details of plans, backup plans, preparations made, perceived control over the impulse, and so forth. Refer the student to inpatient psychiatric treatment as necessary.

21. Use a genogram to identify people with whom the students feel comfortable sharing their feelings (e.g., family members, teachers, counselors, adult neighbors, religious leaders, etc.).

22. Encourage the students to talk with their parents about the traumatic experience and their feelings surrounding the experience.

23. Encourage the students to share with their teachers when their thoughts and feelings about the trauma are interfering with their learning.

24. Assist school personnel in writing a plan for communicating information about the tragedy to the parents, the students, and the community; facilitate policy implementation.

25. Advise the staff to refer to the school's crisis response plan manual for guidelines in writing memos, statements, handouts, media releases, and so forth.

26. Review all informational material to ensure that it is consistent with other information being disseminated.

27. Conduct evening groups for parents in which they discuss their concerns, express their emotional reactions about the trauma, and are provided information about acute and delayed stress reactions in students.

28. Teach the parents the benefits of asking their children daily about their activities of the day and their thoughts experienced throughout the day.

29. Send home with the students, one month following the incident, educational handouts describing the symptoms of acute and delayed stress reactions.

30. Teach the students the benefits of journaling, creating a collage of memories, using art/drawing to communicate with parents and teachers about how they are feeling.

31. Facilitate a critical incident stress debriefing for the school staff to decrease their distress over the event and increase their ability to provide support to the students.

32. Allow time each day for school staff to debrief, to express their emotions, and to realize how this situation has had an impact on them.

33. Sensitize the staff as to how they have been affected by the traumatic event, and redirect the staff when they focus solely on the students' needs.

34. Assign students to write a letter to their deceased peer saying good-bye. Process the students' reactions to the assignment.

35. Assign the students to write about their favorite memory/memories of the deceased to be collected in a book for the deceased's parents.

36. Encourage the staff to return to a normal operating schedule, allowing enough flexibility to be responsive to students' needing to talk about the event.

37. Encourage the parents to communicate to teachers any concerns about what they are seeing at home (and vice versa) in terms of the child's trauma reactions.

38. Utilize the Trauma Symptom Checklist for Adolescents (Briere) weekly to assess delayed reactions to the event.

39. Reaffirm the future to the students and staff. Talk in hopeful terms. Mention positive plans and rebuilding; reinforce any future talk by the students and staff.

40. Assist in planning a memorial commemoration in

honor of the deceased in which the staff and students may take part.

41. Encourage the students and staff to memorialize the deceased with their own expressions of remembrance (e.g., a poem, drawings, flowers, photos, monetary contribution to a cause that the deceased supported, etc.); designate a place for collection of such remembrances.

42. Assist school staff in writing a plan to address the ongoing needs of students, parents, and staff, specifying actions to be taken over the next year such as the distribution of mailings, monitoring for symptoms of delayed stress, referring to appropriate supportive services, and preparing for anniversary reactions.

__. _____

_____

__. _____

_____

__. _____

_____

DIAGNOSTIC SUGGESTIONS

Axis I: V62.3   Academic Problems
308.3   Acute Stress Disorder
309.xx   Adjustment Disorder
305.00   Alcohol Abuse

	V62.82	Bereavement
	300.01	Generalized Anxiety Disorder
	296.2x	Major Depressive Disorder, Single Episode
	307.47	Nightmare Disorder
	313.81	Oppositional Defiant Disorder
	309.81	Posttraumatic Stress Disorder
	309.21	Separation Anxiety Disorder
	_____	_____
	_____	_____
Axis II:	V71.09	No Diagnosis
	_____	_____
	_____	_____

SCHOOL TRAUMA (COLLEGE)

BEHAVIORAL DEFINITIONS

1. The traumatic, sudden death or serious injury of student(s), residence hall advisor(s)/director(s), or faculty member(s) (e.g., due to suicide, motor vehicle accident, homicide/random shooting on campus, dormitory fire, natural disaster, bomb explosion, etc.).
2. Sudden death of a student while participating in an athletic or extracurricular activity.
3. Stalking, kidnapping, or rape on or near the college campus.
4. Dramatic structural damage to dormitory, multistudent facility, or academic building caused by fire, bomb explosion or bomb threat, boiler blowup, chemical infiltration through the heating/cooling system, or a natural disaster (tornado, earthquake, flood).
5. Persistent lack of attendance in classes.
6. Social withdrawal and isolation; avoidance of certain locations/buildings on college campus.
7. Difficulty with sleep and/or nightmares about the traumatic event.
8. Sudden onset or increased use of alcohol or other mood-altering substances.
9. Physical complaints of headaches, nausea, shortness of breath, gastrointestinal problems, loss of appetite, or overeating.
10. Preoccupation with death and/or an increased verbalization of suicidal thoughts.
11. Feelings of irrational guilt regarding having been a survivor of the trauma while others died.
12. Persistent fear of death or personal injury occurring to self.
13. Grief expressed in sadness and tearfulness.

—. _____

_____

—. _____
   _____
   _____

—. _____
   _____

LONG-TERM GOALS

1. Return to pretrauma level of functioning.
2. Reduce the risk of long-term psychological distress.
3. Receive the psychological and social support necessary to adapt to the traumatic event.
4. Grieve and develop healthy coping mechanisms following the traumatic event.
5. Overcome fear of harm, and return to a normal level of functioning.

—. _____
   _____

—. _____
   _____
   _____

—. _____
   _____

SHORT-TERM OBJECTIVES

1. Students, college staff/officials, residence hall advisors/directors, family members, and law enforcement officials provide factual information about the traumatic event. (1, 2)

2. College officials or residence hall advisors/directors identify any missing students. (3)

3. Residence hall advisors/directors identify students who are at high risk for a

THERAPEUTIC INTERVENTIONS

1. Communicate openly with college officials, staff, law enforcement, medical personnel, or the deceased's family, roommate(s), or friends to determine the details or suspected cause of the traumatic event.

2. Encourage college officials to establish a crisis center/phone hotline solely for students involved in the incident to respond to and/or to contact for information.

severe emotional reaction to the trauma. (4, 5, 6)

4. Students needing immediate mental health professional attention access such services. (6, 7)

5. Students describe the facts of the traumatic incident accurately and reject false information. (8, 9)

6. Students express their emotional reactions to the event. (6, 10, 15)

7. Students verbalize an understanding of the causes of their anger related to the incident. (10, 11)

8. Students identify the aspects of the incident that were most disturbing. (12, 13)

9. Students identify the impact that the traumatic event has had upon their daily functioning. (14, 15)

10. Students report the termination of flashbacks. (16, 17)

11. Students remain active and not withdrawn or isolating themselves. (18)

12. Students verbalize a realistic understanding of the cause of the trauma and indicate that blame does not rest with themselves. (19)

13. Students identify any use of alcohol or other substances as a means of coping with the traumatic event. (20, 21)

3. Ask the college officials to retrieve the names of students residing in the dormitory, registered to attend classes in the destroyed academic building, and/ or students identified as victims/witnesses to the trauma.

4. Educate residence hall advisors/directors about high-risk reaction criteria such as any students who: are close friends, roommates, or relatives of the victim; have a history of mental illness; have active suicidal ideation or demonstrate suicidal behaviors; have already experienced a significant loss; have a current pattern or history of excessive substance use; have inadequate or a damaged support system; witnessed the trauma; self-identify as at risk.

5. Utilize psychological tests to assess the mental status of students [e.g., the Beck Depression Scale, the Symptom Checklist 90, or the Trauma Symptom Inventory (Briere)].

6. Assess each student's level of emotional distress to identify those who appear to be a high risk for complications in their reactions and need immediate intervention and/or referral for intensive mental health attention.

14. Students verbalize any thoughts of suicide. (22)

15. Students utilize coping strategies to help them cope with the traumatic event. (23, 24, 25)

16. Students identify people with whom they can trust to share their feelings with about this incident. (26, 27, 28)

17. College personnel write a plan to disseminate information to the students, parents, and the community. (29)

18. College personnel provide accurate and appropriate information to parents, students, and the community according to a written plan. (29, 30, 31)

19. Parents express their thoughts and feelings about the tragedy. (32, 33)

20. College personnel participate in a critical incident stress debriefing. (34, 35)

21. Students say good-bye to their deceased peer. (36, 37)

22. Students discuss the future in positive terms. (38)

23. Students and college personnel attend and participate in a memorial to the deceased. (37, 39, 40)

24. College operations and residence hall operations return to a normal operating schedule. (41)

7. Refer high-risk students to the appropriate mental health professional(s) within the college campus as well as in the community.

8. Ask the students to describe the facts associated with the event and the feelings that they have about it. Normalize feelings of fear, anger, frustration, and grief.

9. Separate the facts of what happened from the false rumors that the students may be hearing.

10. Explore the students' feelings of fear, vulnerability, frustration, or helplessness as causes of angry reactions; encourage acceptance of these feelings as normal rather than becoming angry over them.

11. Probe why, at what, and with whom the student is angry; process the anger to resolution.

12. Ask the students if they could change one aspect of the incident without changing the outcome, what that would be.

13. Probe how this incident relates to something in the students' personal lives that may be causing a magnification of their emotions.

14. Ask the students to identify how the traumatic event has negatively impacted their lives.

25. College staff develop a written plan to address the ongoing needs of the students, parents, and staff. (42)

__. _____
    _____

__. _____
    _____

__. _____
    _____

15. Administer the Trauma Symptom Inventory (Briere) to assess the nature and severity of the emotional, cognitive, and behavioral impact of the trauma.

16. Explore whether the student has had any flashback experiences to this traumatic event.

17. Determine if the student's flashbacks are being triggered by something that reminds him/her of the traumatic event; explain how flashbacks will diminish as the feelings and facts about the trauma are communicated to others.

18. Ask the students to keep an activity log: documenting their time spent alone, on the computer, sleeping, playing video games, socializing, and so forth.

19. Reassure the students that they are not to blame for the deaths of the students or the faculty members; redirect the students to place the blame on the perpetrator.

20. Assess the student for any pattern of alcohol and/or drug abuse. If present, refer him/her to a substance abuse treatment program.

21. Teach the students how using substances to escape or feel numb produces further complications and problems. Offer alternative

coping mechanisms of journaling, exercising, and/or meditation.

22. Conduct a suicide assessment, noting details of plans, backup plans, preparations made, perceived control over the impulse, and so on. Refer the student to inpatient psychiatric treatment as necessary.

23. Teach students the benefits of journaling, creating a collage of memories, using art/drawing to communicate their feelings and emotions.

24. Administer the eye movement desensitization and reprocessing (EMDR) technique to reduce immediate tension.

25. Teach the students relaxation skills, utilizing biofeedback techniques, progressive muscle relaxation, and guided imagery.

26. Use a genogram to identify people with whom the students feel comfortable sharing their feelings (e.g., family members, teachers, counselors, peers, religious leaders, etc.).

27. Encourage the students to talk with their parents about the traumatic experience and their feelings surrounding the experience.

28. Encourage the students to call home three or more times a week for one month to keep communication

open with their parents, decreasing the parents' anxieties and giving the students an avenue of expression.

29. Assist college personnel in writing a plan for communicating information about the tragedy to the parents, the students, and the community; facilitate policy implementation.

30. Advise the staff to refer to the college's crisis response plan manual for guidelines in writing memos, statements, handouts, media releases, and so on.

31. Review all informational material to ensure that it is consistent with other information being disseminated.

32. Conduct evening or weekend groups for parents in which they are told factual information of the event, they can discuss their concerns, express their emotional reactions about the trauma, and are provided educational information about acute and delayed stress reactions in students.

33. Teach the parents the benefits of keeping open communication with their child, encouraging the parents to ask their child about their emotions and thoughts regarding the event and not just ask about the facts of the event or their child's daily activities.

34. Facilitate two separate critical incident stress debriefings—one for the college administration and one for the residence hall advisors/directors—to decrease their distress over the event and increase their ability to provide support to the students.

35. Sensitize the staff as to how they have been affected by the traumatic event, and redirect the staff when they focus solely on the students' needs.

36. Assign students to write a letter to their deceased peer saying good-bye. Process the students' reactions to the assignment.

37. Assign the students to write about their favorite memory/memories of the deceased to be collected in a book for the deceased's parents.

38. Reaffirm the future to the students and college personnel. Talk in hopeful terms. Mention positive plans and rebuilding; reinforce any future talk by the students and staff.

39. Assist in planning a memorial commemoration in honor of the deceased in which the staff and students may take part.

40. Encourage the students and staff to memorialize the deceased with their

own expressions of remembrance (e.g., a poem, drawings, flowers, photos, monetary contribution to a cause that the deceased supported, etc.); designate a place for collection of such remembrances.

41. Encourage the college administration and residence hall advisor/director to return to a normal operating schedule, allowing enough flexibility to be responsive to students' needing to talk about the event.

42. Assist the college staff in writing a plan to address the ongoing needs of students, parents, and staff, specifying actions to be taken over the next year such as the distribution of mailings, monitoring for symptoms of delayed stress, referring to appropriate supportive services, and preparing for anniversary reactions.

___. _____

_____

___. _____

_____

___. _____

_____

DIAGNOSTIC SUGGESTIONS

Axis I: V62.3   Academic Problem
             308.3   Acute Stress Disorder
             309.xx   Adjustment Disorder

	305.00	Alcohol Abuse
	V62.82	Bereavement
	296.xx	Bipolar I Disorder
	300.02	Generalized Anxiety Disorder
	296.2x	Major Depressive Disorder, Single Episode
	307.47	Nightmare Disorder
	304.80	Polysubstance Dependence
	309.81	Posttraumatic Stress Disorder
	_____	_____
	_____	_____
Axis II:	301.82	Avoidant Personality Disorder
	301.83	Borderline Personality Disorder
	301.9	Personality Disorder NOS
	799.9	Diagnosis Deferred
	_____	_____
	_____	_____

SCHOOL TRAUMA (STAFF)

BEHAVIORAL DEFINITIONS

1. The traumatic, sudden death or serious injury of student(s) or faculty member(s) [e.g., due to suicide, motor vehicle accident, homicide, sudden infant death syndrome (SIDS), school bus tragedy, playground incident, natural disaster, bomb explosion, etc.).
2. Death of a student or faculty member who had a prolonged illness.
3. Sudden death of a student while participating in an athletic or extracurricular activity.
4. Stalking or child kidnapping in the vicinity of the school.
5. An outsider who is in the building, threatening violence to anyone.
6. Dramatic school damage caused by fire, bomb explosion or bomb threat, boiler blowup, chemical infiltration through the heating/cooling system, or a natural disaster (tornado, earthquake, flood).
7. Sense of helplessness, feeling out of control, emotional numbness, avoiding contact with others, loss of motivation, feelings of inadequacy, and/or guilt.
8. Headaches, nausea, shaking/tremors, fatigue, intestinal upset, diarrhea, increased blood pressure, change in appetite, or exhaustion.
9. Experiencing flashbacks, replaying the event over and over in the mind, sense of unreality or disbelief, impaired memory, short attention span, angry thoughts, and/or increased worry.
10. Withdrawing from social, recreational, and/or occupational activities.
11. Increased use of alcohol or drugs.
12. Preoccupation with death and/or an increased verbalization of suicidal thoughts.
13. Feelings of irrational guilt regarding having been a survivor of the trauma while others died.
14. Persistent fear of death or personal injury occurring to self.

—. _____
_____
—. _____
_____
—. _____
_____

LONG-TERM GOALS

1. Return to pretrauma level of functioning.
2. Reduce the risk of long-term psychological distress.
3. Gain an understanding of the traumatic event and its impact upon cognitive, behavioral, physical, and emotional functioning.
4. Diminish flashbacks, intrusive images, and distressing emotional reactions regarding the traumatic event.
5. Grieve and develop healthy coping mechanisms following the traumatic event.
6. Overcome the fear of harm, and return to a normal level of functioning.

—. _____
_____
—. _____
_____
—. _____
_____

SHORT-TERM OBJECTIVES	THERAPEUTIC INTERVENTIONS
1. Describe the traumatic event, providing as much detail as comfort allows. (1, 2, 3, 4)	1. Actively build the level of trust with the client through consistent eye contact, unconditional positive regard, and warm acceptance to help increase his/her ability to identify and express feelings.
2. Describe the feelings that were experienced at the time of the trauma. (4, 5, 6, 7)	

3. Identify the impact that the traumatic event has had on daily functioning. (7, 8, 9)

4. Identify the aspects of the incident that were most disturbing for him/her. (9, 10, 11, 12)

5. Identify distorted cognitive messages that promote fear, and replace those messages with reality-based self-talk that nurtures confidence and calm. (12, 13)

6. Verbalize an increased understanding of the beliefs and images that produce fear, worry, or anxiety. (14, 15)

7. Verbalize an understanding of the causes of anger related to the incident. (15, 16)

8. Report the termination of flashbacks. (14, 17, 18)

9. Report a reduction of sleep disturbance, distressing dreams, or fear of sleeping. (19, 20)

10. Identify use of alcohol or other substances as a means of coping with the traumatic event. (21)

11. Increase the frequency and depth of social activity with friends or family. (22, 23, 24)

12. Return to open communication with family, friends, and coworkers. (24, 25, 26)

13. Avoid and/or minimize contact with media, community members, and others who

2. Gently and sensitively explore the recollection of the facts of the traumatic incident.

3. Ask the client to describe the facts associated with the event and the thoughts that he/she has about it. Separate the facts of what happened from the rumors that the client may be hearing.

4. Prompt the client to describe his/her traumatic experience noting whether he/she is overwhelmed with emotions.

5. Explore the client's emotional reactions (fear, guilt, helplessness, shock, etc.) following the traumatic event.

6. Using a list of common acute stress reactions, ask the client to identify those reactions they are experiencing.

7. Administer the Trauma Symptom Inventory (Briere) to assess the nature and severity of the emotional, cognitive, and behavioral impact of the trauma.

8. Ask the client to identify how the traumatic event has negatively impacted his/her life.

9. Explore what about this incident reminds the client of a similar/previous incident. Assess for possible transference of unresolved feelings from a previous incident onto this incident.

inquire about the incident. (27, 28)

14. Participate in a critical incident stress debriefing. (29, 30, 31)

15. Implement behavioral coping strategies that reduce stress and tension. (32, 33, 34, 35)

16. Attend the funeral of a student or coworker who has died. (36)

17. Attend and participate in a memorial to the deceased. (37, 38)

18. Design an activity to be implemented on the anniversary day of the event or around major life events (i.e., holidays, graduation). (39, 40)

19. Return to a normal operating schedule. (41)

—. _____
   _____

—. _____
   _____

—. _____
   _____

10. Ask the client if he/she could change one aspect of the incident without changing the outcome, what that would be.

11. Probe how this incident relates to something in the client's personal life that may be causing a magnification of the emotions.

12. Explore distorted cognitive messages that mediate negative emotional reactions to the trauma.

13. Help the client develop reality-based cognitive messages that will increase self-confidence and facilitate a reduction in the fight-or-flight response.

14. Have the client write in a journal the recurring images or memories associated with the trauma.

15. Explore the client's feelings of fear, vulnerability, frustration, or helplessness as causes of angry reactions; encourage acceptance of these feelings as normal rather than becoming angry over them.

16. Probe why, at what, and with whom the client is angry; process the anger to resolution.

17. Explore whether the client has had any flashback experiences to this incident or previous traumatic events.

18. Determine if the client's flashbacks are being trig-

gered by something that reminds him/her of the traumatic event; explain how flashbacks will diminish as the feelings and facts about the trauma are communicated to others.

19. Assign the client homework of keeping a journal of dreams, nightmares, and disturbing thoughts that are affecting his/her sleep patterns. Process the journal information in session.

20. Process the client's fear of sleeping as possibly a result of having nightmares or of having to face reality when he/she wakes up.

21. Complete a substance abuse evaluation, and refer the client to substance abuse treatment as appropriate.

22. Educate the client of the psychological consequences of social isolation, and encourage him/her to increase his/her level of activity.

23. Assist the client in identifying social activities that were a source of pleasure prior to the incident, and encourage him/her to resume these activities.

24. Encourage the client to attend at least two social events with family or friends.

25. Conduct a conjoint session with the client's spouse/family to facilitate effective communication skills.

26. Encourage the client to talk with peers, supervisors, or his/her spouse about the thoughts and emotions he/she has been experiencing since the incident.

27. Educate the client about the psychological consequences (feelings of helplessness, guilt, loss of confidence in work abilities, etc.) of continued exposure to the incident precipitated by contact with reporters, community members, and others who want to discuss the incident. Encourage the client to avoid these people.

28. Role-play with the client how he/she will politely respond to those in the community asking questions that he/she does not want to answer.

29. Contact a local critical incident stress management (CISM) team to provide a critical incident stress debriefing (CISD).

30. Contact the International Critical Incident Stress Foundation (ICISF) to find a local CISM team.

31. Encourage participation in a CISD that is facilitated by an ICISF-trained debriefer.

32. Assist the client in developing behavioral coping strategies (i.e., increased social involvement, journaling, and/or physical exercise) that will ameliorate the stress reactions.

33. Administer the eye movement desensitization and reprocessing (EMDR) technique to reduce immediate tension.

34. Teach the client relaxation skills utilizing biofeedback techniques, progressive muscle relaxation, and/or guided imagery techniques.

35. Encourage the use of strenuous physical exercise alternating with relaxation to alleviate physical stress reactions.

36. Encourage the client to attend the funeral of the student(s) or his/her deceased coworker to facilitate the grieving process. Explore his/her reactions afterward in session.

37. Ask the client to write about his/her favorite memory/memories of the deceased to be collected in a book for the deceased's spouse/parents.

38. Encourage the client to memorialize the deceased with his/her own expressions of remembrance (e.g., a poem, drawings, flowers, photos, monetary contribution to a cause that the deceased supported, etc.); designate a place for collection of such remembrances.

39. Prompt the client to talk about how the pain, sense of loss, or alteration of life resulting from the traumatic event has increased

with the approaching anniversary day of the event or other trigger events (e.g., holidays, vacation, graduation, etc.).

40. Teach the client about the possible increase in emotional disturbance that is associated with the anniversary date or other significant days that trigger memories of the event; develop coping techniques or rituals to decrease anniversary reactions.

41. Encourage the client to return to a normal operating schedule, allowing enough flexibility to be responsive to their own emotional and physical needs.

__. _____
_____

__. _____
_____

__. _____
_____

DIAGNOSTIC SUGGESTIONS

Axis I:	308.3	Acute Stress Disorder
	309.xx	Adjustment Disorder
	305.00	Alcohol Abuse
	V62.82	Bereavement
	296.xx	Bipolar I Disorder
	300.4	Dysthymic Disorder
	300.02	Generalized Anxiety Disorder
	296.xx	Major Depressive Disorder
	V62.2	Occupational Problems

304.80   Polysubstance Dependence
309.81   Posttraumatic Stress Disorder

———   ————————————

Axis II: 301.82   Avoidant Personality Disorder
301.83   Borderline Personality Disorder
301.50   Histrionic Personality Disorder
301.9   Personality Disorder NOS

———   ————————————
———   ————————————

SEXUAL ASSAULT/RAPE

BEHAVIORAL DEFINITIONS

1. Self-report of being forced into sexual activity with another person.
2. Injuries (e.g., abrasions, bruises, cuts, venereal disease, etc.) that give evidence of the sexual assault.
3. Avoidance of activities, locations, and circumstances associated with the assault.
4. Afraid to be in public places or crowds alone.
5. Recurrent intrusive memories, nightmares, and/or thoughts of the assault.
6. Subjective experience of anxiety, helplessness, fear, or irritability since the assault.
7. Restricted range of affect, subjective sense of numbing, and/or not "feeling real."
8. Feeling of vulnerability, powerlessness, guilt, or shame.
9. Insomnia, difficulty concentrating, and motor restlessness.

—. _____
_____

—. _____
_____

—. _____
_____

LONG-TERM GOALS

1. Return to the level of occupational, psychological, and social functioning present before the assault.
2. Eliminate intrusive memories, thoughts, and nightmares of the assault.

3. Engage in a range of social activities that are a source of pleasure and satisfaction.
4. Engage in satisfying sexual intercourse.
5. Assimilate the rape experience, and place it into perspective.

—. _____
   _____
   _____

—. _____
   _____
   _____

—. _____
   _____

SHORT-TERM OBJECTIVES

1. Give an accurate description of the assault. (1, 2)

2. File a report with law enforcement. (3)

3. Verbalize emotional reactions to the rape, including guilt, helplessness, anger, anxiety, and/or self-blame. (2, 4, 5)

4. Receive necessary medical care to treat any injuries. (6)

5. Consent to the completion of the Sexual Assault Evidence Kit. (3, 6)

6. Verbalize any suicidal or homicidal ideation, and contract not to harm self or others. (7)

7. Describe how the rape has affected psychological and social functioning. (8, 9, 10)

8. Cooperate with psychological testing to determine the severity of the impact of the rape. (10)

THERAPEUTIC INTERVENTIONS

1. Develop a rapport with the client by providing unconditional positive regard, asking open-ended questions, and maintaining a nonjudgmental attitude.

2. Conduct a comprehensive assessment of the rape, including the time of day, location, sex and race of the rapist, and any previous history of victimization.

3. Refer the client to a local police agency or sexual assault crisis center.

4. Explore the client's emotional reactions to the assault, and encourage the expression of all emotions.

5. When the client expresses guilt/self blame, redirect the client to view the rape as a crime committed against him/her for which the rapist is to blame.

9. Comply with an evaluation for psychotropic medication. (11)

10. Identify any substances that are being used to cope with the emotional consequences of the rape. (12, 15)

11. Abstain from the use of all illegal drugs and alcohol while in treatment. (13, 14, 15)

12. Describe the goals of treatment in behavioral terms. (16, 17)

13. Attend a self-defense class to increase feelings of self-confidence and mastery. (18)

14. Identify people who can be relied upon for emotional support. (19, 20, 22)

15. Write a plan to engage other people for emotional support. (21, 22)

16. Attend a rape victim support group. (22)

17. Verbalize any feelings of guilt or shame about not resisting the assault enough. (23, 24)

18. Write a plan of action to be taken to create safety. (18, 25)

19. Verbalize an understanding of the emotional and psychological impact of rape. (26, 27)

20. List situations, locations, and/or people that have been avoided since the rape. (28)

6. Refer the client to a medical doctor or a sexual assault crisis center for an evaluation, and monitor his/her compliance with the assessment and treatment recommendations.

7. Conduct a crisis assessment regarding any suicidal and homicidal ideations. Have the client sign a contract not to harm himself/herself or others. If the client is unable to contract for his/her safety, refer him/her to inpatient psychiatric treatment.

8. Obtain a complete biopsychosocial history describing the client's previous level of functioning in relationships, work, and so on before the rape. Inquire as to recent changes in overall functioning.

9. Ask the client how his/her life has changed since the assault.

10. Complete Briere's Trauma Symptom Inventory to determine the severity of the impact of the rape.

11. Refer the client to a physician or psychiatrist for a psychotropic medication evaluation for the treatment of anxiety, depression, sleeplessness, and so on, and monitor his/her compliance with the physician's orders.

12. Conduct a substance abuse assessment including types

21. Arrange avoided situations in a hierarchy according to how much they subjectively cause distress. (29, 30)

22. Practice relaxation techniques. (31)

23. Practice imaginal exposure to the rape. (32)

24. Listen to audiotaped descriptions of the assault. (33)

25. Confront avoided situations. (32, 33, 34, 35)

26. Challenge cognitive distortions related to the rape, and replace them with more realistic beliefs. (36)

27. Practice thought-stopping techniques to decrease intrusive thoughts and ruminations. (37)

28. Stop blaming self for the rape. (5, 24, 38)

29. Verbalize a rejection of the misconception that the rape happened to him/her for a reason or as a result of something he/she did. (5, 24, 38)

30. Resume previously enjoyed social activities. (19, 20, 21, 39, 40)

31. Verbalize a willingness to begin to engage in intimacy and sexual intercourse. (41, 42)

32. Report positive emotional experiences when engaging in consensual sexual intercourse. (42, 43, 44)

of substances being used, the frequency and amount of use, and any legal or social consequences of use.

13. Ask the client for a commitment to abstain from the use of all drugs/alcohol during treatment.

14. Refer the client to a 12-step program for assistance with maintaining sobriety.

15. Refer the client to a substance abuse program for ongoing treatment and random drug testing.

16. Assist the client in describing the goals of treatment in behavioral terms.

17. Using a solution-focused approach, ask the client the miracle question: "If the problem that brought you to treatment were to miraculously be solved over night, how would you know?"

18. Refer the client to self-defense classes to increase his/her sense of mastery and decrease his/her feelings of vulnerability.

19. Assist the client in drawing an eco-map to graphically depict available social/emotional support. Probe the client regarding a full range of possibilities, including friends, family, religious leaders, coworkers, neighbors, class mates, and so on.

20. Inquire as to the client's social support system, and as-

—. _____
     _____

—. _____
     _____

—. _____
     _____

sist with identifying people on whom he/she can rely.

21. Assist the client in writing a social interaction plan that includes time spent with supportive people. Monitor progress with implementing the plan.

22. Refer the client to a rape victim support group.

23. Teach the client how fear inhibits people from fighting back when threatened, and help him/her realize that his/her survival was the most important issue.

24. Educate the client that rape is an aggressive, hostile act of violence rather than a sexual act; affirm the client's decisions in the face of reasonable fear.

25. Assign the client homework of writing things that he/she can do to protect himself/ herself. Monitor progress in implementing this plan.

26. Educate the client about the psychosocial impact of rape, including a description of common reactions (e.g., difficulty sleeping, avoidance of activities associated with the rape, numbing, and anxiety).

27. Assign the client to read *After Silence: Rape and My Journey Back* (Raine).

28. Assist the client in preparing a list of situations and places that have been avoided since the rape.

29. Have the client list avoided situations in a hierarchy from the most disturbing to the least.

30. Using a scaling method, have the client scale each avoided situation from 1 to 100, with 100 being *overwhelming anxiety.*

31. Teach the client relaxation techniques: deep-breathing exercises, progressive muscle relaxation, cue-controlled relaxation, and differential relaxation.

32. Have the client induce relaxation and then recall the rape. Continue until the client reports that the image is less anxiety provoking; audiotape his/her description of the rape.

33. Assign the client homework of listening to his/her audiotaped description of the assault to increase desensitization to the rape.

34. Use systematic desensitization techniques to reduce the client's anxiety associated with the ranked elements of the rape situation.

35. Have the client begin to visit some of the previously avoided situations (at first in the company of a supportive person if necessary, then alone). Process his/her reactions to the intervention in session.

36. Teach the client how to use an automatic thought

record to identify and track distorted cognitions about the rape; challenge and replace the cognitive distortions related to the rape.

37. Educate the client regarding thought-stopping techniques, including saying no when intrusive thoughts are present and snapping a rubber band on his/her wrist.

38. Confront the client when he/she takes responsibility for the assault, and assist him/her with placing blame on the rapist.

39. Encourage the client to seek out increased social activity.

40. Assist the client in developing a system of self-reward for progress toward socialization goals (e.g., buying a special gift, eating a dessert, etc.).

41. Encourage the client to openly communicate with his/her sex partner his/her difficulties with intimacy/sexual relations.

42. Assign the client to keep a journal of thoughts and emotions when sexually aroused with a consensual partner.

43. Process with the client the emotions and thoughts experienced when he/she is engaged in consensual intimate/sexual relations.

44. Train the client in the use of desensitization tech-

niques when he/she is en-
gaged in sexual intimacy.

___. _____
   _____

___. _____
   _____

___. _____
   _____

DIAGNOSTIC SUGGESTIONS

Axis I: 308.3   Acute Stress Disorder
             309.24   Adjustment Disorder with Anxiety
             309.0   Adjustment Disorder with Depressed Mood
             309.28   Adjustment Disorder with Mixed Anxiety and
                        Depressed Mood
             300.6   Depersonalization Disorder
             300.12   Dissociative Amnesia
             300.4   Dysthymic Disorder
             296.xx   Major Depressive Disorder
             V61.1   Partner Relational Problem
             995.81   Physical Abuse of Adult (Victim)
             309.81   Posttraumatic Stress Disorder
             995.81   Sexual Abuse of Adult (Victim)

             _____   _____

Axis II: 301.83   Borderline Personality Disorder
             301.6   Dependent Personality Disorder
             301.50   Histrionic Personality Disorder
             301.0   Paranoid Personality Disorder

             _____   _____
             _____   _____

STALKING VICTIM

BEHAVIORAL DEFINITIONS

1. Experience of repeated or continuing harassment.
2. Contact from another individual that is initiated or continued without consent, or in disregard of own expressed desire that the contact be avoided or discontinued.
3. Has received one or more credible threats against self, a member of the family, or another individual living in the household.
4. Movements inside and/or outside of the home have been monitored.
5. An unwanted person spying on actions, conversations, and paths of travel.
6. Harassment, unexplained phone calls, insignificant personal or home property tampered with for no apparent reason.
7. Feelings of terror, persecution, intimidation, paranoia, or entrapment.
8. Has changed daily routines (e.g., route taken to work/school) to determine if stalking is occurring.
9. Difficulty falling asleep, loss of appetite, homicidal/suicidal ideation, decreased sense of trust.

__. _____
_____
_____

__. _____
_____
_____

__. _____
_____

LONG-TERM GOALS

1. Take legal steps necessary to guarantee safety such as filing a personal restraining order and establishing a plan of escape/safety.
2. Develop the skills necessary to maintain physical and emotional safety in current and future relationships.
3. Return to the level of psychological, emotional, social, and occupational functioning present before the stalking began.

—. _____
   _____

—. _____
   _____

—. _____
   _____

SHORT-TERM OBJECTIVES

1. Describe the history, nature, and intensity of the stalking. (1, 2)
2. Verbalize emotional reactions to the stalking. (3, 4)
3. Describe how the stalking has affected psychological and social functioning. (2, 3, 4, 5)
4. Cooperate with psychological testing to determine the severity of the impact of the stalking. (4)
5. Identify the individual(s) who may be stalking. (2, 6)
6. Write a safety plan that will be implemented to establish and maintain physical safety. (7)
7. File a personal restraining order (PRO). (8)

THERAPEUTIC INTERVENTIONS

1. Develop a rapport with the client by providing unconditional positive regard, asking open-ended questions, and maintaining a supportive, nonjudgmental attitude.
2. Gather a history of the stalking, determining when the stalking began, situations that occurred prior to the start of the stalking, and the impact of the stalking upon personal, social, and professional activities.
3. Explore the client's emotional reaction to the stalking.
4. Complete the Trauma Symptom Inventory (Briere) to determine the severity of the impact of the stalking.

8. Cooperate with law enforcement and their investigation. (9, 10)

9. Change daily routines to decrease the likelihood of the stalker knowing whereabouts. (11, 12, 13, 14)

10. List five ways to increase safety in the home. (15, 16)

11. In a public place, confront the stalker, and request the stalking to stop. (17, 18)

12. Attend a self-defense class to increase feelings of self-confidence and mastery. (19)

13. Enlist the support of coworkers, relatives, and friends. (20, 21, 22, 23, 24)

14. Move to a safe living environment. (23, 24, 25)

15. Challenge cognitive distortions related to the stalking, and replace them with more realistic beliefs. (26, 27)

16. Verbalize an understanding that the stalking is the responsibility of the stalker. (26, 28, 29)

17. Verbalize increased self-confidence. (30)

—. _____
   _____

—. _____
   _____

—. _____
   _____

5. Ask the client how her/his life has changed since the stalking started.

6. Review with the client relationships that have ended and the circumstances surrounding these relationships to assist him/her in identifying possible stalking suspects.

7. Assist the client in developing a written safety plan that details what actions [e.g., filing a personal restraining order (PRO), using alternate routes for transportation, cooperating with law enforcement, confronting the stalker in the presence of support, etc.] will be taken to establish and maintain physical and emotional safety.

8. Assist the client in filing a PRO against the individual who is suspected of stalking.

9. Encourage the client to file a police report.

10. Suggest that the client work collaboratively with law enforcement. Confront any resistance such as fear of disclosing personal information, feelings of hopelessness, and so on by reminding the client of the need to establish and maintain his/her safety.

11. Assign the client to complete a time study of his/her daily actions for a week. Review this in session, making

suggestions for unpre-
dictable alterations to
his/her schedules.

12. Ask the client to list the activities, associations, and
groups that he/she attends
regularly. Assess if there
are options to attend these
activities at different times.

13. Assist the client in identifying alternative routes to
school, work, and other activities. Encourage him/her
to use these alternative
routes to increase safety.
Monitor the client's compliance in using the alternative routes.

14. Develop a strategic plan of
not adhering to a daily routine. Encourage leaving/
arriving home at different
times; use different roadways to travel to/from work/
school; have visitors to the
house and stay overnight so
as to not consistently be
home alone.

15. Walk through the client's
home, identifying ways that
he/she can make his/her
home more secure.

16. Assist the client in identifying five ways to increase
safety in the home, such as
installing dead-bolt locks,
keeping curtains drawn,
purchasing a cordless/
wireless phone, identifying
an escape route, and/or installing a security system in
his/her home for greater security.

17. Role-play with the client ways to approach the stalker in a public place and with supportive people present; request the stalking to stop. Process his/her reactions to the role-play situation.

18. Teach the client assertiveness techniques to be able to approach the stalker in a public domain and, with confidence, tell the stalker to stop the stalking and leave him/her alone.

19. Refer the client to self-defense classes, tae-bo, or karate classes to increase a sense of mastery and self-confidence, and decrease feelings of vulnerability.

20. Offer a family session to have the client communicate to his/her family or friends the danger he/she is in. Elicit the family/friends support.

21. Ask the client to solicit the support of his/her employer, employee assistance program, and security officers at work to keep the client safe while working.

22. In a conjoint session, educate family/friends on ways they can protect the client, the need to contact law enforcement, and assess their own safety.

23. Assist the client in identifying friends or family who would be willing and able to

provide a safe, protected living situation.

24. Encourage the client to move in with friends, family, coworkers, and so forth, until safety is established.

25. Inquire as to the client's and other household members' safety in each session; if a threat of harm exists, arrange for escape to a safe living situation (i.e., women's crisis center).

26. When the client expresses guilt/self-blame, redirect the client to view the stalking as a crime committed against him/her for which the stalker is to blame.

27. Teach the client how to use an automatic thought record to identify and track distorted cognitions about the stalking; challenge and replace the cognitive distortions related to the stalking.

28. Confront and challenge any of the client's minimizing regarding the seriousness of the abuse. Assess if the client believes he/she is to blame for the stalking.

29. Confront the client about making excuses for the stalker's actions, minimizing its impact, or accepting blame for it.

30. Verbally reinforce the client's use of positive statements regarding self-confidence and accomplishments.

—. _____
    _____
—. _____
    _____
—. _____
    _____

DIAGNOSTIC SUGGESTIONS

Axis I: 308.3   Acute Stress Disorder
              309.24   Adjustment Disorder with Anxiety
              309.0   Adjustment Disorder with Depressed Mood
              309.28   Adjustment Disorder with Mixed Anxiety and
                         Depressed Mood
              300.4   Dysthymic Disorder
              296.xx   Major Depressive Disorder
              V65.2   Malingering
              V61.1   Partner Relational Problem
              309.81   Posttraumatic Stress Disorder
              295.70   Schizoaffective Disorder

              _____   _____

              _____   _____

Axis II: 301.83   Borderline Personality Disorder
              301.6   Dependent Personality Disorder
              301.0   Paranoid Personality Disorder

              _____   _____

              _____   _____

SUDDEN/ACCIDENTAL DEATH (ADULT)

BEHAVIORAL DEFINITIONS

1. Sudden death of a person as a result of a motor vehicle accident, shooting/homicide, assault and battery, drowning, or fire entrapment.
2. Intense emotional, physical, or behavioral reactions experienced by the family/friends.
3. Shock reactions as evidenced by denial, confusion, poor concentration, inability to make decisions, diaphoresis, shaking, or fainting.
4. Emotional reactions of crying, hysteria, disbelief, or anger.
5. Behavioral reactions of agitation, aggressive actions, tense muscles, social withdrawal, or fetal position posture.

___. _____
   _____

___. _____
   _____

___. _____
   _____

LONG-TERM GOALS

1. Develop healthy coping strategies following a sudden, traumatic death.
2. Begin the grieving process.
3. Accept the loss realistically, and overcome shock or denial.
4. Return to previous level of social, physical, emotional, and spiritual functioning.
5. Healthy assimilation of this event into the daily functioning of the family/friends.

—. _____
_____
_____

—. _____
_____
_____

—. _____
_____
_____

SHORT-TERM OBJECTIVES

1. Verbalize an understanding that the loved one has died. (1, 2, 3)

2. Verbalize an understanding of the cause(s) of death and the circumstances surrounding it. (4, 5, 6)

3. Verbalize an understanding of the rescue/lifesaving attempts that took place. (5, 6)

4. Identify the activities and/or health of the deceased for the preceding 24 hours. (7, 8)

5. Verbalize the lifestyle and hobbies of the deceased. (8, 9)

6. Obtain social support from neighbors, family, or friends to prevent isolation after professional staff contact. (10, 11)

7. Identify and utilize spiritual sources of support. (12, 13, 14)

8. Receive medical treatment for any injuries and/or com-

THERAPEUTIC INTERVENTIONS

1. Establish a rapport by maintaining eye contact with the clients, speaking clearly and slowly, and from the same position (e.g., sitting or standing) as the clients.

2. Identify who the immediate family and/or friends are, and congregate them in a secure, private room/area to communicate the death notification.

3. Inform the client(s) that their loved one is dead (using the words *dead* or *died*), and allow for silence following the death notification.

4. Explore with the family/friends what they know of the traumatic incident/event.

5. Obtain a copy of the police record or medical record of the event. Review the entire report with the family/friends, offering pauses to determine how the family/

plications in reaction to the traumatic news. (15)

9. Verbalize any assaultive ideations. (16)

10. Abstain from any violent or aggressive behavior. (16, 17, 18)

11. Openly describe all emotional and behavioral reactions experienced. (19, 20, 21)

12. Verbalize an increased understanding of the grief process. (19, 21, 22, 23, 24)

13. Stop blaming self for the loss. (24, 25)

14. Verbalize a decrease in anger toward the medical staff. (26, 27)

15. Verbalize an understanding of psychological complications that would require additional treatment. (28)

16. Participate in psychological evaluation and treatment. (29, 30, 31)

17. View the deceased's body. (32, 33, 34, 35)

18. Say good-bye to the deceased. (36, 37)

19. Visit the scene of the loved one's traumatic death. (38, 39, 40, 41)

20. Identify ways to minimize reexposure to traumatic memories. (39, 42)

21. Identify the funeral home, burial arrangements, and memorial service. (43)

friends are absorbing the information.

6. Assist the family/friends in obtaining details of the traumatic event, including lifesaving measures, from medical professionals and/ or a law enforcement officer.

7. Ask the family/friends to recall the activities/health of the deceased over the past 24 hours.

8. Ask the family/friends to share their recent memories of the deceased.

9. Conduct a brief psychosocial assessment to determine the lifestyle, occupation, values, activities, and so on of the deceased. Reflect on this information in a supportive way during crisis intervention.

10. Assist in determining with the family/friends the people they feel should be contacted about the death.

11. Assist the family/friends in making phone calls to nearby relatives/friends to inform them of the sudden death; encourage these people to get together with the family/friends immediately.

12. Inquire about the clients' religious/spiritual beliefs, and encourage the family/friends to use this resource for support.

13. Arrange for a clergy or religious leader to visit the clients at the hospital,

22. Decide whether to participate in organ donation. (44, 45, 46)

23. Leave the hospital, or site, within a reasonable amount of time. (47)

24. Share the pain of loss with significant others. (10, 11, 48)

25. Share memories of the deceased. (49, 50)

26. Report competency in managing the household, bills, domestic tasks, and so on. (51, 52)

27. Report a consumption of a healthy diet. (53)

28. Report an adequate amount of refreshing sleep. (54)

29. Decrease the time spent daily focused on the loss. (55)

30. Watch videos on the theme of grief and loss to compare personal experience with that of characters in the movies. (56)

31. Attend a bereavement support group. (57)

32. Attend a victim support group. (57)

__. _____
   _____

__. _____
   _____

__. _____
   _____

home, site, or some suitable location.

14. Offer prayer or ask for a chaplain to offer prayer for strength and guidance of the family/friends.

15. Facilitate the client's access to emergency medical services or medical personnel as needed for complaints of chest pain or other emergency medical conditions.

16. Assess the clients for an urge to react violently to medical staff, or others who were involved with the traumatic death, and deescalate verbally.

17. Contact law enforcement or trained individuals who can help behaviorally manage the enraged family/friends.

18. Notify any intended victims of the clients as mandated by legal requirements.

19. Normalize the clients' experience by informing them that a wide range of emotional reactions (crying, numbness, shock, etc.) are normal, common, and to be expected.

20. Encourage the expression of emotions by asking open-ended questions, providing tissues for tears, and reassuring that all reactions are appropriate.

21. Educate the client(s) that keeping pent-up feelings has the potential of only growing stronger and be-

coming more destructive with time.

22. Educate the client(s) on the stages of grief (e.g., denial, anger, bargaining, depression, and acceptance).

23. Reassure the client(s) that grief is personal and that everyone differs in the way it is processed.

24. Assign the client to read *When Bad Things Happen to Good People* (Kushner) or *How Can It Be All Right When Everything Is All Wrong?* (Smedes).

25. Redirect the client from self-blame by reminding them of the medical reasons for the loss.

26. Gently confront the family/friends regarding any misdirected anger (e.g., toward the medical staff, self, others, etc.). Remind them of the stages of grieving.

27. Interpret anger at the medical staff as a symptom of feeling helpless. Process reactions to the interpretation in session.

28. Educate the client(s) about possible psychological complications to this traumatic loss that would require more treatment (e.g., flashbacks, suicidal ideation, etc.).

29. Conduct a comprehensive mental status evaluation, including previous episodes of mood disorder, history of psychiatric hospitalizations

and counseling services, other losses, and severity of current mood disorder.

30. Conduct psychological tests [e.g., Symptom Checklist 90 (SCL-90) or the Beck Depression Inventory] to identify the severity of the depressed mood.

31. Refer the client to a psychologist or social worker, and monitor his/her compliance with the treatment recommendations. [See the chapters entitled "Depression," "Posttraumatic Stress Disorder (PTSD)" and/or "Acute Stress Disorder" in this Planner.]

32. Inquire from law enforcement/medical staff as to the appearance of the deceased's body.

33. Inform the client(s) about the condition of the body (i.e. missing limbs, blood, etc.) to prepare them psychologically.

34. Physically and emotionally support the immediate family/friends in viewing the deceased's body.

35. Educate the family/friends that by viewing the deceased in the environment of his/her death prevents distorted images that may develop in the future about how the person died.

36. Encourage the client(s) to talk to the deceased, and say good-bye.

37. Assign the client to write a letter to the deceased, saying good-bye. Process the client's reaction to the assignment.

38. If the deceased's body is unable to be viewed for investigative reasons or because of its grotesque condition, support the family/friends in going to the location of the traumatic death after the body has been removed.

39. Inform the family/friends that exposure to the location of the traumatic death in the future will likely produce strong emotions and memories.

40. Accompany the family/friends to the site of the traumatic death of their loved one; process emotional reactions on-site.

41. Provide an area for the family/friends to pace and move about that does not disturb the integrity of the crime scene or residence.

42. Encourage rerouting a usual path of travel to avoid the location of the traumatic event, especially early in the grieving process.

43. Facilitate the client's making decisions and arrangements related to funeral home selection, crematorium, burial, and/or a memorial service.

44. Educate the client(s) about organ donation, including

that the deceased's body will not be disfigured, there is no cost to the family, and what organs are viable for donation.

45. Inquire about any religious or psychological objections to organ donation.

46. Contact the regional organ procurement agency for consent/information on the donation of the deceased's organs.

47. Using a solution-focused approach, ask the family/ friends how they will know when it is time to leave the body behind and return home. Assist them in completing any tasks that prevent them from leaving comfortably.

48. Remind the family/friends that grieving will continue after leaving the hospital, and encourage the family/ friends to use previously identified sources of support.

49. Using a special photo album, have the client organize a creative memory album and bring it to a session for sharing.

50. Ask the client to bring to a session wedding albums, degrees, awards, and such, and have the client share the story behind each represented achievement of the deceased's.

51. Encourage the client to cope with forgetfulness and pre-

occupation that are associated with traumatic grief by
using a calendar to record
appointments, due dates of
bills, children's activities,
and other important dates.

52. Urge the client to stay organized by using a numbered
expand folder to keep track
of bills, messages, activities,
appointments, and the like.

53. Educate the client about
healthy eating, in spite of
the desire to avoid food
while grieving (i.e., eat in
small amounts four or more
times a day; avoid food that
is high in fat or cholesterol;
avoid alcohol and caffeine).

54. Inquire about the client's
sleeping patterns, and encourage using journaling to
record thought preoccupa-
tions that present difficulty
with falling asleep or staying asleep; process journal
material in sessions.

55. Suggest that the client set
aside a specific time-limited
period each day to focus on
mourning the loss (i.e., 20
minutes each morning).
After the time period is up,
the client will go on with
regular daily activities with
an understanding that
he/she will put aside the
mourning feelings that occur
throughout the day until the
next scheduled time.

56. Ask the client to watch
films such as *Terms of En-*

dearment, On Golden Pond, Ordinary People, or similar films that focus on loss and grieving. Discuss with the client how the characters cope with loss and express their grief.

57. Educate the client about community resources (e.g., bereavement support groups, victim witness programs, etc.).

___. _____

_____

___. _____

_____

___. _____

_____

DIAGNOSTIC SUGGESTIONS

Axis I: 308.3   Acute Stress Disorder
              309.xx   Adjustment Disorder
              V62.82   Bereavement
              296.2x   Major Depressive Disorder, Single Episode
              300.01   Panic Disorder without Agoraphobia
              309.21   Separation Anxiety Disorder
              _____   _____

Axis II: 301.6   Dependent Personality Disorder
              301.9   Personality Disorder NOS
              _____   _____
              _____   _____

SUDDEN/ACCIDENTAL DEATH (CHILD)

BEHAVIORAL DEFINITIONS

1. Sudden death of a child as a result of a motor vehicle accident, poisonous ingestion, shooting/homicide, drowning, suffocation, or fire entrapment.
2. Sudden death of a child resulting from sudden infant death syndrome (SIDS).
3. Shock reactions as evidenced by denial, confusion, poor concentration, inability to make decisions, diaphoresis, shaking, or fainting.
4. Emotional reactions of crying, hysteria, disbelief, or anger.
5. Behavioral reactions of agitation, aggression, tense muscles, clinging to a possession of the child, or social withdrawal.
6. Physical reactions of weakness, fatigue, shortness of breath, loss of appetite, headache, nausea, and/or dizziness.

—. _____
   _____
   _____
—. _____
   _____
   _____
—. _____
   _____

LONG-TERM GOALS

1. Stabilization of emotional, behavioral, and physical status.
2. Develop healthy coping strategies following the sudden/traumatic death of the child.
3. Begin the grieving process.
4. Accept the loss realistically, and overcome shock or denial.

5. Return to previous level of social, physical, emotional, and spiritual functioning.
6. Healthy assimilation of this traumatic event into the daily functioning of the parents/family.

—. _____
_____
_____

—. _____
_____
_____

—. _____
_____
_____

SHORT-TERM OBJECTIVES

1. Verbalize an understanding that the child has died. (1, 2, 3)
2. Verbalize an understanding of the cause(s) of death and the circumstances surrounding it. (4, 5, 6)
3. Verbalize an understanding of the rescue/lifesaving attempts that took place. (5, 6)
4. Recall the activities and/or health of the deceased child for the preceding 24 hours. (7, 8)
5. Verbalize the lifestyle, interests, and strengths of the child. (8, 9)
6. Obtain social support from neighbors, family members, or friends of the family to prevent isolation after professional staff contact. (10, 11)

THERAPEUTIC INTERVENTIONS

1. Establish a rapport by maintaining eye contact with the parents, speaking clearly and slowly, and from the same position, (e.g., sitting or standing) as the parents.
2. Identify who the parents and immediate family are, and congregate them in a secure, private room/area to communicate the death notification.
3. Inform the parents that their child is dead (using the words _dead_ or _died_), and allow for silence following the death notification.
4. Explore with the parents/ caretakers what they know of the traumatic incident/ event.
5. Obtain a copy of the police record or medical record of the event. Review the entire

7. Family members openly share their grief and support. (11)

8. Identify and utilize spiritual sources of support. (12, 13, 14)

9. Receive medical treatment for any injuries and/or complications in reaction to the traumatic news. (15)

10. Verbalize any assaultive ideations. (16)

11. Abstain from any violent or aggressive behavior. (16, 17, 18)

12. Openly describe all emotional and behavioral reactions experienced. (19, 20, 21)

13. Verbalize an increased understanding of the grief process. (19, 21, 22, 23, 24)

14. The parents or caretaker stop blaming self for the loss. (24, 25)

15. Verbalize a decrease in anger toward the medical staff. (26, 27)

16. Verbalize an understanding of the psychological complications that would require additional treatment. (28)

17. Participate in a psychological evaluation and treatment. (29, 30, 31)

18. View and/or hold the deceased child. (32, 33, 34, 35)

19. Say good-bye to the child. (36, 37)

report with the parents, offering pauses to determine how they are absorbing the information.

6. Assist the parents in obtaining details of the traumatic event, including lifesaving efforts, from medical professionals and/or a law enforcement officer.

7. Ask the parents to recall the activities/health of the child over the past 24 hours.

8. Ask the parents to share their recent memories of the child.

9. Conduct a brief psychosocial assessment to determine the lifestyle, education, values, activities, and so forth of the child. Reflect on this information in a supportive way during crisis intervention.

10. Assist the parents in making phone calls to nearby relatives/friends to inform them of the sudden death; encourage these people to get together with the parents immediately.

11. Hold a family session where the parents and family members share their feelings of grief/loss.

12. Inquire about the parents' religious/spiritual beliefs, and encourage them to use this resource for support.

13. Arrange for a clergy or religious leader to visit the parents at the hospital, home, or some suitable location.

20. Visit the location where the child's traumatic death occurred. (38, 39, 40, 41)

21. Identify ways to minimize reexposure to traumatic memories. (39, 42)

22. Identify the funeral home, burial arrangements, and memorial service. (43)

23. Decide whether to participate in organ donation. (44, 45, 46)

24. Leave the hospital, or death site, within a reasonable amount of time. (47)

25. Openly share memories of the child. (48, 49)

26. Verbalize the grief of lost opportunities for the child and the family. (50)

27. Report organizing the child's room, packaging clothes and toys. (51, 52)

28. Report consumption of a healthy diet. (53)

29. Report an adequate amount of refreshing sleep. (54)

30. Decrease the amount of time spent daily focused on the loss. (55)

31. Watch videos on the theme of grieving for a child, and compare personal experiences with that of characters in the movies. (56)

32. Attend a SIDS or bereavement support group. (57)

—. _____
   _____

14. Offer prayer or ask for a chaplain to offer prayer for strength and guidance of the parents.

15. Facilitate the parents' access to emergency medical services or medical personnel as needed for complaints of chest pain or other emergency medical conditions.

16. Assess the parents for an urge to react violently toward the caretaker, medical staff, or others who were involved with the traumatic death, and deescalate verbally.

17. Contact law enforcement or trained individuals who can help behaviorally manage the enraged parents.

18. Notify any intended victims of the parents as mandated by legal requirements.

19. Normalize the parents' reactions by informing them that a wide range of emotional reactions (crying, numbness, anger, shock, etc.) are normal, common, and to be expected.

20. Encourage the expression of emotions by asking open-ended questions, providing tissues for tears, and offering reassurance that all feelings are understandable.

21. Educate the parents that unexpected feelings have the potential of growing

__. _____
    _____
__. _____
    _____

stronger and becoming
more destructive with time.

22. Educate the parents on the
stages of grief (e.g., denial,
anger, bargaining, depression, and acceptance).

23. Reassure the parents that
grief is personal and that
everyone differs in the way
it is processed.

24. Assign the parents to read
*When Bad Things Happen
to Good People* (Kushner),
The Bereaved Parent
(Schiff), or *A Child Dies: A
Portrait of Family Grief*
(Hagan Arnold).

25. Redirect the parents/
caretakers from self-blame
by reminding them of the
medical or accidental reasons for the loss.

26. Gently confront the parents
regarding any misdirected
anger (e.g., toward the medical staff, self, caretakers,
others, etc.). Remind them
of the stages of grieving.

27. Interpret anger at the medical staff as a symptom of
feeling helpless. Process reactions to the interpretation
in session.

28. Educate the parents about
possible psychological complications to this traumatic
loss that would require
more treatment (e.g., flashbacks, unresolved depres-
sion, suicidal ideation, etc.).

29. Conduct a comprehensive
mental status evaluation,

including previous episodes of mood disorder, history of psychiatric hospitalizations and counseling services, other losses, and the severity of the current mood disorder.

30. Conduct psychological tests [e.g., Symptom Checklist 90 (SCL-90) or the Beck Depression Inventory] to identify the severity of the depressed mood.

31. Refer the parents to a psychologist or social worker, and monitor compliance with treatment recommendations. [See the chapters entitled "Depression," "Posttraumatic Stress Disorder (PTSD)," and/or "Acute Stress Disorder" in this Planner.]

32. Inquire from law enforcement/medical staff as to the appearance of the child's body.

33. Inform the parents about the condition of the child's body (i.e., missing limbs, blood, skin discoloration, etc.) to prepare them psychologically.

34. Physically and emotionally support the parents in viewing and/or holding the child's body.

35. Educate the parents that by viewing the child in the environment of his/her death prevents distorted images that may develop in the fu-

ture about how the child died.

36. Encourage the parents to talk to the deceased child, share their dreams, and say good-bye.

37. Assign the parents to write a letter to the child, saying good-bye. Process their reactions to the assignment.

38. If the child's body is unable to be viewed for investigative reasons or because of its grotesque condition, support the parents in going to the location of the traumatic death after the body has been removed.

39. Inform the parents that exposure to the location of the traumatic death in the future will likely produce strong emotions and memories.

40. Accompany the parents to the site of the their child's traumatic death; process emotional reactions on-site.

41. Provide an area for the parents to pace and move about that does not disturb the integrity of the crime scene or residence.

42. Encourage rerouting a usual path of travel to avoid the location of the traumatic event, especially early in the grieving process.

43. Facilitate the parents in making decisions and arrangements related to funeral home selection,

crematorium, burial, and/or a memorial service.

44. Educate the parents about organ donation, including that the child's body will not be disfigured, that there is no cost to the family, and what organs are viable for donation.

45. Inquire about any religious or psychological objections to organ donation.

46. Contact the regional organ procurement agency for consent/information on the donation of the child's organs.

47. Using a solution-focused approach, ask the parents how they will know when it is time to leave their deceased child and return home. Assist them in completing any tasks that prevent them from leaving comfortably.

48. Encourage the parents to create a creative memory album dedicated to the child through use of photos or other memorabilia.

49. Ask the parents to bring to a session yearbooks, degrees, awards, and so on, and have the parents share the story behind the child's achievement.

50. Explore what future plans were imagined for the child and the family; empathize with the lost dreams.

51. Explore the parents' need to clean their child's room,

take care of the belongings, distribute their clothes and toys, and so on. Encourage them to perform these functions gradually to avoid feeling overwhelmed or regretting decisions that cannot be reversed.

52. Process the pain associated with organizing their child's room, boxing up their child's belongings, and such.

53. Educate the parents about healthy eating (i.e., eat in small amounts four or more times a day; avoid food that is high in fat or cholesterol; avoid alcohol and caffeine); encourage food intake even though grief reduces appetite.

54. Inquire about the parents' sleeping patterns, and encourage using journaling of thoughts and feelings to reduce difficulties in falling asleep or staying asleep.

55. Suggest that the parents set aside a specific time-limited period each day to focus on mourning the loss (e.g., 20 minutes each morning). After the time period is up, ask the parents to go on with their regular daily activities with an understanding that they will put aside the mourning feelings that occur throughout the day until the next scheduled time.

56. Ask the parents to watch films (e.g., *Ordinary People*)

that focus on loss and grieving. Discuss with the parents how those characters cope with loss and express their grief.

57. Educate the parents about community resources such as SIDS support groups, bereaved parents support groups, parents of murdered children support groups, and so forth.

__. _____

_____

__. _____

_____

__. _____

_____

DIAGNOSTIC SUGGESTIONS

Axis I:	308.3	Acute Stress Disorder
	309.xx	Adjustment Disorder
	V62.82	Bereavement
	296.2x	Major Depressive Disorder, Single Episode
	300.01	Panic Disorder without Agoraphobia
	309.21	Separation Anxiety Disorder
	_____	_____
	_____	_____
Axis II:	301.6	Dependent Personality Disorder
	301.9	Personality Disorder NOS
	_____	_____
	_____	_____

SUICIDE (ADULT)

BEHAVIORAL DEFINITIONS

1. Suicide of a spouse.
2. Suicide of an extended family member or friend.
3. Behavioral reactions of agitation, aggression, tense muscles, clinging on to a possession of the deceased's, and/or social withdrawal.
4. Shock reactions as evidenced by denial, confusion, poor concentration, inability to make decisions, diaphoresis, shaking, or fainting.
5. Emotional reactions of crying, hysteria, disbelief, or anger.
6. Physical reactions of weakness, shortness of breath, chest pain/pressure, headaches, nausea, and/or diarrhea.

—. _____
   _____
   _____
—. _____
   _____
   _____
—. _____
   _____

LONG-TERM GOALS

1. Develop a healthy grieving process following the suicide of a person.
2. Accept the person's death realistically, and overcome shame, guilt, or denial.
3. Return to previous level of social, physical, emotional, and spiritual functioning.
4. Healthy assimilation of this event into the daily functioning of the client's family.

—. _____

_____

—. _____

_____

—. _____

_____

SHORT-TERM OBJECTIVES

1. Verbalize an understanding that the person has committed suicide. (1, 2, 3, 4)

2. Share the suicide note in session. (5)

3. Recall the emotions, activities, and changes in behavior/moods that the person demonstrated in the past 72 hours. (6, 7, 8)

4. Openly describe all emotional and behavioral reactions experienced. (1, 8, 9)

5. Stop blaming self for the suicide. (2, 6, 7, 10)

6. Verbalize a resolution of survivor guilt feelings. (10, 11, 12, 13)

7. Abstain from seeking answers to the question, Why did the person commit suicide? (11, 14, 15)

8. Utilize religious support to cope with the suicide. (16)

9. Verbalize an increased understanding of the grief process. (17, 18)

10. Verbalize what to tell friends, family, and the

THERAPEUTIC INTERVENTIONS

1. Establish a rapport by maintaining eye contact with the client(s), speaking clearly and slowly, and from the same position, (e.g., sitting or standing) as the client(s).

2. Inform the client that the person has committed suicide. Provide him/her with corroborating reports (e.g., police reports, medical records, etc.) that provide information about the cause of the person's death.

3. Explore with the client(s) what he/she knows of the situation surrounding the death of the deceased.

4. Confront denial of the suicide by reviewing the facts of the death with the client(s).

5. Read the suicide note with the client(s), and provide emotional support as it is analyzed for dysfunctional thinking, blaming, hurt, and/or anger.

community about the nature of the person's death. (19, 20, 21)

11. Verbalize any thoughts of suicide. (22, 23, 24)

12. Identify feelings of depression or complicated bereavement. (24, 25)

13. Report nightmares, intrusive memories/images, and/or hallucinations of the deceased. (26, 27)

14. Verbalize a decrease in misdirected angry feelings. (28, 29, 30)

15. Openly share memories of the deceased. (30, 31)

16. Say good-bye to the deceased. (32, 33)

17. Identify the funeral home, burial arrangements, and memorial service. (34)

18. Decrease the amount of time spent daily focused on the loss. (35)

19. Develop a plan to cope with the economic consequences of the suicide. (36, 37, 38)

20. Attend a support group for survivors of suicide. (39)

__. _____
    _____
__. _____
    _____
__. _____
    _____

6. Ask the client(s) to recall if he/she noticed any changes in the deceased's demeanor, behaviors, attitudes, or emotions over the past 72 hours; process feelings of "I should have seen this coming."

7. Review with the client(s) the deceased's mental status, activities, and other cues that the person was depressed prior to the suicide (such as social withdrawal, conflict with peers, etc.); resolve feelings of self-recrimination for not predicting the suicide.

8. Normalize the client's reactions by informing him/her that a wide range of emotional reactions (guilt, crying, shame, numbness, shock, etc.) are normal, common, and to be expected.

9. Encourage the expression of emotions by asking open-ended questions, providing tissues for tears, and offering reassurance for all appropriate reactions.

10. Confront the client when he/she takes responsibility for the suicide. Review the facts surrounding the suicide.

11. Explore with the client his/her regrets by asking about what he/she believes could have, should have, or would have been done.

Redirect him/her to focus on the facts surrounding the person's suicide, and educate him/her that ruminating over what if's is perpetuating feelings of guilt.

12. Ask the client to recall the last time he/she saw or spoke to the deceased. Encourage the client to share what was said.

13. Explore with the client what he/she wished had been said to the deceased before the suicide. Utilize the empty-chair technique (Perls) to facilitate this discussion.

14. Redirect the client from finding the answer to *why* to the facts of the suicide and the actual behaviors/ reactions that were demonstrated by the deceased.

15. Acknowledge the client's perceived need to answer the question *why* while gently pointing out the only one who knows that answer is dead.

16. Inquire about the client's religious/spiritual beliefs, and encourage him/her to use this resource for support. Call upon the client's personal faith to assist with grieving.

17. Educate the client on the stages of grief (e.g., denial, anger, bargaining, depression, and acceptance).

18. Assign the client to read *When Bad Things Happen to Good People* (Kushner) and/or *Getting to the Other Side of Grief: Overcoming the Loss of a Spouse* (Zonnebelt-Smeenge and DeVries).

19. Inquire as to what the client wants to tell friends, family, and the community about the person's death. Assist him/her in identifying advantages and disadvantages to full disclosure.

20. Explore with the client any cultural/religious barriers (e.g., inability to bury the person on sacred grounds, family dishonor, etc.) to telling people that the person committed suicide.

21. Role-play with the client disclosing information about the person's death to different people in the community. Process the reaction to the exercise.

22. Conduct a suicide assessment, noting details of the plan, backup plans, preparations made, perceived control over the impulse, and so forth.

23. Have the client sign a contract agreeing not to harm himself/herself. Detail what actions are to be taken by the client if he/she is experiencing suicidal urges (calling 911, going to the nearest emergency room, calling the therapist, etc.).

24. Utilize a psychological test (e.g., Beck Depression Inventory or the Symptom Checklist 90) to assess the severity of the client's depression.

25. Differentiate for the client the difference between "normal" grief and complicated bereavement (the level of guilt reported, suicidal ideation, morbid preoccupations, hallucinations, and/or prolonged or marked functional impairments).

26. Conduct a thought disorder assessment. Determine if the auditory and/or visual hallucinations of the deceased are a normal grief reaction or one of disturbed, psychotic thinking.

27. Ask the client to report in detail the images or voices that he/she reports seeing/ hearing. Have the client keep a journal of the images/ voices, noting his/her thoughts or actions before the hallucination occurred.

28. Gently confront the client regarding any misdirected anger (e.g., toward the deceased's friends, God, the mental health system, etc.). Remind him/her of the stages of grieving and how feeling angry is one of those phases.

29. Interpret for the client the feelings of anger as a symptom of feeling helpless. Edu-

cate the client on the self-
focus of suicide and how
suicidal people intentionally
push away those who love
them.

30. Ask the client to describe
the happy, sad, and angry
memories they have of the
person. Process the memo-
ries and the pain of those
memories.

31. Conduct a family session in
which all members share
their memories of the de-
ceased and their emotional
reactions to the suicide.

32. Utilize symbolic healing
tactics (e.g., sending balloons up in the sky to represent letting go).

33. Assign the client to write a
letter to the person, saying
good-bye. Process their reactions to the assignment.

34. Facilitate the client in making decisions and arrangements related to funeral
home selection, cremato-
rium, burial, and/or a
memorial service.

35. Suggest that the client set
aside a specific time-limited
period each day to focus on
mourning the loss (e.g., 20
minutes each morning).
After the time period is up,
the client will go on with
his/her regular daily activities with an understanding
that they will put aside the
mourning feelings that
occur throughout the day

until the next scheduled time.

36. Inquire as to the economic impact of the suicide (e.g., loss of income from spouse, difficulty paying bills, mortgage, etc.).

37. Assist the client in identifying sources of economic support (e.g., life insurance, friends and family, government entitlement programs, etc.).

38. Assign the client homework of writing a detailed plan on how to meet economic needs (e.g., selling the house, obtaining employment, etc). Review plan with the client in session.

39. Refer the client to a support group for survivors of suicide, such as Compassionate Friends or Survivors of Suicide.

__. _____
    _____
__. _____
    _____
__. _____
    _____

DIAGNOSTIC SUGGESTIONS

Axis I: 308.3   Acute Stress Disorder
               309.xx   Adjustment Disorder
               V62.82   Bereavement
               296.xx   Bipolar I Disorder

	300.4	Dysthymic Disorder
	296.xx	Major Depressive Disorder
	_____	_____
	_____	_____
Axis II:	301.83	Borderline Personality Disorder
	301.9	Personality Disorder NOS
	_____	_____
	_____	_____

SUICIDE (CHILD)

BEHAVIORAL DEFINITIONS

1. Suicide of own child.
2. Suicide of a student, youth athlete, or neighbor child.
3. Behavioral reactions of agitation, aggression, tense muscles, clinging to a possession of the child's, and/or social withdrawal.
4. Shock reactions as evidenced by denial, confusion, poor concentration, inability to make decisions, diaphoresis, shaking, or fainting.
5. Emotional reactions of crying, hysteria, disbelief, or anger.
6. Physical reactions of weakness, shortness of breath, chest pain/ pressure, headaches, nausea, and/or diarrhea.

__. _____
_____
__. _____
_____
__. _____
_____

LONG-TERM GOALS

1. Develop a healthy grieving process following the suicide of a child.
2. Accept the child's death realistically, and overcome shame, guilt, or denial.
3. Return to previous level of social, physical, emotional, and spiritual functioning.
4. Healthy assimilation of this event into the daily functioning of the parent(s)/family.

—. _____
    _____
    _____
—. _____
    _____
    _____
—. _____
    _____
    _____

SHORT-TERM OBJECTIVES

1. Verbalize an understanding that the child has committed suicide. (1, 2, 3, 4)

2. Share a suicide note that was left. (5, 6)

3. Verbalize an understanding of the message and the deeper meaning of the suicide note. (7, 8)

4. Recall the emotions, activities, and changes in behavior/mood that the child demonstrated in the past 72 hours. (9, 10)

5. Openly describe all emotional and behavioral reactions experienced. (1, 10, 11, 12)

6. Stop blaming self for the suicide. (2, 7, 13, 14, 15)

7. Verbalize resolution of feelings of survivor guilt. (9, 10, 15, 16, 17)

8. Abstain from seeking answers to the question, Why did the child commit suicide? (18, 19, 20, 21)

THERAPEUTIC INTERVENTIONS

1. Establish a rapport by maintaining eye contact with the parent(s), speaking clearly and slowly, and from the same position, (e.g., sitting or standing) as the parent(s).

2. Inform the parent(s) that their child has committed suicide. Provide them with corroborating reports (e.g., police reports, medical records, etc.) that provide information about the cause of the child's death.

3. Explore with the parent(s) what they know of the situation surrounding the death of the child.

4. Confront the parent's/parents' denial of the suicide by reviewing the facts of the child's death.

5. Read the suicide note with the parent(s), and provide emotional support.

6. Analyze the handwriting of the suicide note and the self-focused language, pen-

9. Verbalize an increased understanding of the grief process. (22, 23)

10. Verbalize what to tell friends, family, and the community about the nature of the child's death. (24, 25, 26)

11. Verbalize any thoughts of suicide. (27, 28)

12. Identify feelings of depression or complicated bereavement. (29, 30)

13. Report nightmares, intrusive memories/images, and/or hallucinations of the deceased child. (31, 32, 33)

14. Verbalize a decrease in misdirected angry feelings about the suicide. (34, 35, 36, 37)

15. Openly share memories of the child. (38, 39, 40)

16. Identify the loss of hopes, dreams, and expectations for the child and the family. (41, 42)

17. Say good-bye to the child. (42, 43, 44)

18. Identify the funeral home, burial arrangements, and memorial service. (25, 45)

19. Decrease the amount of time that is spent daily focused on the loss. (46)

20. Begin the process of disposing of the child's belongings. (47, 48)

21. Attend a support group for survivors of suicide. (48)

manship, and/or altered reasoning in the thinking of the child.

7. Identify whom the child is blaming in the suicide note, and challenge the client to not accept the blame. Help the client to understand the child's individual choice to kill himself/herself and how the person identified as being blamed is not responsible.

8. Ask the parent(s) to identify what isn't being blatantly stated in the suicide note; to "read between the lines," to encounter the hurt, depression, pain, and anger the child must have been feeling.

9. Ask the parent(s) to recall if they noticed any changes in the child's demeanor, behaviors, attitudes, or emotions over the past 72 hours; process feelings of "I should have seen this coming."

10. Review with the parent(s) the child's mental status, activities, and other cues that the child was depressed prior to the suicide (such as social withdrawal, conflict with peers, etc.); resolve feelings of self-recrimination for not predicting the suicide.

11. Normalize the parent's/ parents' reactions by informing them that a wide

___. _____
   _____
   _____
___. _____
   _____
___. _____
   _____

range of emotional reactions (guilt, crying, shame, numbness, shock, etc.) are normal, common, and to be expected.

12. Encourage the expression of emotions by asking open-ended questions, providing tissues for tears, and offering reassurance for all appropriate reactions.

13. Confront the parent(s) when they take responsibility for the suicide. Review the facts surrounding the suicide.

14. Educate the parent(s) on the self-focus of suicide and how no one person influences or causes another's choice of suicide.

15. Explore with the parent(s) their regrets by asking about what they believe they could have, should have, or would have done differently. Redirect them to focus on the facts surrounding their child's suicide, and educate them that ruminating over what if's is perpetuating their feelings of guilt.

16. Ask the parent(s) to recall the last time they saw or spoke to their child. Encourage them to share what was said.

17. Explore with the parent(s) what they wished they had a chance to say to their child before the suicide. Utilize the empty-chair tech-

nique (Perls) to facilitate this discussion.

18. Redirect the parent's/parents' thinking from finding the answer to *why* to the facts of the suicide and the actual behaviors/reactions that were demonstrated by the child.

19. Encourage the parent(s) to move toward no longer needing the answer to the question *why* and to being partially satisfied with the answers/facts they do know.

20. Acknowledge the parent's/parents' perceived need to answer the question *why* while gently pointing out the only one who knows that answer completely is dead.

21. Inquire about the parent's/parents' religious/spiritual beliefs, and encourage them to use this resource for support. Call upon their personal faith to assist with their grieving.

22. Educate the parent(s) on the stages of grief (e.g., denial, anger, bargaining, depression, and acceptance).

23. Assign the parent(s) to read *When Bad Things Happen to Good People* (Kushner), *The Bereaved Parent* (Schiff), *A Child Dies: A Portrait of Family Grief* (Hagan Arnold).

24. Inquire as to what the parent(s) want to tell friends,

family, and the community about the child's death. Assist them in identifying advantages and disadvantages to full disclosure.

25. Explore with the parent(s) any cultural barriers (e.g., inability to bury the child on sacred grounds, family dishonor, etc.) to telling people that the child committed suicide.

26. Role-play with the parent(s) disclosing information about the child's death to different people in the community. Process their reaction to the exercise.

27. Conduct a suicide assessment, noting details of the plan, backup plans, preparations made, perceived control over the impulse, and so on.

28. Have the parent(s) sign a contract agreeing not to harm himself/herself. Detail what actions are to be taken by the parent(s) if they are experiencing suicidal urges (calling 911, going to the nearest emergency room, calling the therapist, etc.).

29. Utilize a psychological test (e.g., Beck Depression Inventory or the Symptom Checklist-90) to assess the severity of the parent's/parents' depression.

30. Differentiate for the parent(s) the difference between "normal" grief and compli-

cated bereavement (the level of guilt reported, suicidal ideation, morbid preoccupations, hallucinations, and/or prolonged and marked functional impairments).

31. Conduct a thought disorder assessment. Determine if the auditory and/or visual hallucinations of the deceased child are a normal grief reaction or one of disturbed, psychotic thinking.

32. Ask the parent(s) to report in detail the images or voices they report to be seeing/hearing. Have the parent(s) keep a journal of the images/voices, noting their thoughts or actions before the hallucination occurred.

33. Explore if the intrusive images are produced by the parent(s) as a comfort measure, as a result of denial of the child's death, or as a means of feeling like they are keeping the child alive by creating such in their thinking.

34. Gently confront the parent(s) regarding any misdirected anger (e.g., toward the child's friends, God, the other parent, the mental health system, etc.). Remind them of the stages of grieving and how feeling angry is one of those phases.

35. Interpret for the parent(s) the feelings of anger as a

symptom of feeling helpless. Educate them on the self-ishness of suicide and how suicidal people intentionally push away those who love them.

36. Assess if the parent's/parents' anger is turning into bitterness and/or hostility. Confront them regarding this observation.

37. Explore if the parent's/parents' anger is at the child's selfishness, giving up the fight to live, or a reaction of disbelief that the parents didn't know their child as well as they thought they did.

38. Ask the parent(s) to describe the happy, sad, and angry memories they have of the child. Process the memories and the pain of those memories.

39. Ask the parent(s) to bring to a session yearbooks, degrees, awards, and such, and have them share the story behind the achievements of the child.

40. Conduct a family session in which all members share their memories of the deceased and their emotional reactions to the suicide.

41. Explore what future plans were imagined for the child and the family; empathize with the lost dreams.

42. Encourage the parent(s) to talk to the deceased child,

share their dreams, and say good-bye; utilize an empty-chair technique (Perls).

43. Utilize symbolic healing tactics (e.g., sending balloons up in the sky to represent letting go).

44. Assign the parent(s) to write a letter to the child, saying good-bye. Process their reactions to the assignment.

45. Facilitate the parent(s) in making decisions and arrangements related to funeral home selection, crematorium, burial, and/or a memorial service.

46. Suggest that the parent(s) set aside a specific time-limited period each day to focus on mourning the loss (e.g., 20 minutes each morning). After the time period is up, the parent(s) will go on with their regular daily activities with an understanding that they will put aside the mourning feelings that occur throughout the day until the next scheduled time.

47. Explore the parent's/parents' need to clean their child's room, take care of the belongings, distribute their clothes, and so on. Encourage them to perform these functions gradually to avoid feeling overwhelmed or regretting decisions that cannot be reversed.

48. Refer the parent(s) to a support group for survivors of suicide, such as Compassionate Friends or Survivors of Suicide.

__. _____
   _____

__. _____
   _____

__. _____
   _____

DIAGNOSTIC SUGGESTIONS

Axis I:	308.3	Acute Stress Disorder
	309.xx	Adjustment Disorder
	V62.82	Bereavement
	296.xx	Bipolar I Disorder
	300.4	Dysthymic Disorder
	296.xx	Major Depressive Disorder
	_____	_____
	_____	
Axis II:	301.83	Borderline Personality Disorder
	301.9	Personality Disorder NOS
	_____	_____
	_____	_____

WORKPLACE VIOLENCE

BEHAVIORAL DEFINITIONS

1. Physical assault of an employee at work.
2. Shooting, robbery, or other violent crime committed at the workplace.
3. Subjective experience of intense fear, helplessness, or horror.
4. Recurrent, intrusive, traumatic memories, nightmares, and/or hallucinations related to the crime.
5. Experiences dissociative symptoms of numbing, detachment, derealization, depersonalization, amnesia, or reduction of awareness to surroundings.
6. Marked avoidance of stimuli that arouse recollections of the trauma, whether through thoughts, feelings, conversations, activities, places, or people.
7. Absenteeism, tardiness, and/or self-report of discomfort/emotional distress while at the work site.
8. Symptoms of increased arousal such as difficulty sleeping, irritability, poor concentration, hypervigilance, exaggerated startle response, motor restlessness.

__. _____
   _____

__. _____
   _____

__. _____
   _____

LONG-TERM GOALS

1. Return to regular work schedule and activities.
2. Stabilize physical, cognitive, behavioral, and emotional reactions while increasing the ability to function on a daily basis.
3. Diminish intrusive images and the alteration in functioning or activity level that is due to stimuli associated with the trauma.
4. Assimilate the traumatic event into life experience without ongoing distress.
5. Confront, forgive, or accept the perpetrator of the workplace violence.

—. _____
_____
_____

—. _____
_____
_____

—. _____
_____

SHORT-TERM OBJECTIVES

1. Describe any bodily injury or physical symptom that has resulted from the trauma. (1).
2. Describe the violence witnessed or experienced in the workplace, providing as much detail as comfort allows. (2, 3, 4, 5)
3. Describe the nature of the relationship with the assaultive, violent coworker. (6)
4. Participate in a critical incident stress debriefing (CISD). (7, 8, 9)
5. Identify the impact that the violent event has had on daily functioning. (10, 11)

THERAPEUTIC INTERVENTIONS

1. Make a referral to a physician for a medical evaluation.
2. Actively build the level of trust with the client in individual sessions through consistent eye contact, unconditional positive regard, and warm acceptance to help increase his/her ability to identify and express feelings.
3. Gently and sensitively explore the recollection of the facts of the violence witnessed or experienced in the workplace.

6. Identify distorted cognitive messages that promote fear, and replace those messages with reality-based self-talk that nurtures confidence and calm. (12, 13)

7. Report the termination of flashback experiences. (14, 15, 16)

8. Cooperate with psychological testing to determine the severity of the impact of the event. (17, 18)

9. Take medications as prescribed, and report any side effects to appropriate professions. (19, 20)

10. Implement behavioral coping strategies that reduce tension. (21)

11. Decrease symptoms of autonomic arousal by learning and implementing relaxation techniques. (22, 23, 24, 25)

12. Share thoughts and feelings regarding the traumatic incident with coworkers. (26, 27)

13. Increase time spent at work. (28, 29)

14. Employer implements changes in the work environment that will assist in preventing future incidents. (30, 31)

15. Verbalize an increased sense of safety and security at work. (30, 31, 32)

16. Attend trauma survivor's support group. (33)

4. Explore the client's emotional reaction at the time of the trauma.

5. Consult with law enforcement, relatives, or coworkers who have facts/details regarding the violent experience, to corroborate and/or elaborate on the client's recall.

6. Inquire as to the nature of the relationship with the assaultive/violent coworker (e.g., supervisor, friend, etc.).

7. Contact a local critical incident stress management (CISM) team to provide a critical incident stress debriefing (CISD).

8. Contact the International Critical Incident Stress Foundation (ICISF) to find a local CISM team.

9. Encourage participation in a CISD that is facilitated by an ICISF-trained debriefer.

10. Ask the client to identify how the violent event has negatively impacted his/her life.

11. Administer psychological testing to assess the nature and severity of the emotional, cognitive, and behavioral impact of the trauma.

12. Explore distorted cognitive messages that mediate negative emotional reactions to the trauma.

13. Help client develop reality-based cognitive messages that will increase self-

—.   _____
     _____
     _____
—.   _____
     _____
     _____
—.   _____
     _____

confidence and facilitate a reduction in fight-or-flight response.

14. Explore whether the client has had any flashback experiences to this trauma or previous traumatic events.

15. Prompt the client to describe the violence witnessed or experienced within the session, noting whether he/she is overwhelmed with emotions.

16. Have the client write in a journal the recurring images or memories associated with the violent event.

17. Complete the Trauma Symptom Inventory (Briere), the Beck Depression Scale, or the Symptom Checklist 90 to determine the severity of the impact of the trauma.

18. Assess the client for a mood disorder (e.g., depression or anxiety disorder). (See the chapters entitled "Depression" or "Anxiety" in this Planner.)

19. Refer the client to a psychiatrist or physician for a medication evaluation.

20. Monitor the client's medication compliance and effectiveness. Confer with the psychiatrist or physician regularly.

21. Assist the client in developing behavioral coping strategies (i.e., increased social involvement, journal-

ing, and/or physical exercise) that will ameliorate the stress reactions.

22. Train the client in guided imagery techniques that induce relaxation.

23. Train the client in progressive muscle relaxation procedure.

24. Utilize biofeedback techniques to facilitate the client learning relaxation skills.

25. Conduct eye movement desensitization and reprocessing (EMDR).

26. Gather small groups of coworkers to share their perceptions of the incident; correct any misperceptions and beliefs.

27. In small groups, facilitate coworkers' sharing of their emotional reactions to the incident; explore for successful coping strategies.

28. Encourage the client to return to the work routine; if necessary, phase into these activities gradually but steadily.

29. Go with the client to the scene of the event while offering desensitization techniques to reduce stress reactions as they develop.

30. Facilitate a discussion between staff and management regarding the incident. Focus the discussion upon developing new security measures that would assist

in preventing future incidents (e.g., installing metal detectors and panic buttons, hiring security guards, and performing criminal investigations of applicants for positions, etc.).

31. Using a solution-focused approach, ask the client what needs to happen to feel safe at work. Encourage the client and employer to implement these changes.

32. Monitor the client's adjustment to the work setting after the violent incident; provide support and encouragement.

33. Refer the client to a survivors' support group that is focused on the nature of the trauma to which the client was exposed.

__. _____

_____

__. _____

_____

__. _____

_____

DIAGNOSTIC SUGGESTIONS

Axis I:	308.3	Acute Stress Disorder
	309.24	Adjustment Disorder with Anxiety
	309.0	Adjustment Disorder with Depressed Mood
	309.28	Adjustment Disorder with Mixed Anxiety and Depressed Mood
	300.6	Depersonalization Disorder
	300.12	Dissociative Amnesia

	300.14	Dissociative Identity Disorder
	296.2x	Major Depressive Disorder, Single Episode
	V62.2	Occupational Problems
	309.81	Posttraumatic Stress Disorder
	_____	_____
	_____	_____
Axis II:	301.4	Obsessive-Compulsive Personality Disorder
	301.9	Personality Disorder NOS
	_____	_____
	_____	_____

Appendix A

BIBLIOTHERAPY SUGGESTIONS

Acute Stress Disorder

Beck, A., and G. Emery (1985). *Anxiety Disorders and Phobias: A Cognitive Perspective.* New York: Basic Books.

Bourne, E. (1995). *The Anxiety and Phobia Workbook.* Oakland, CA: New Harbinger Publications.

Craske, M., and D. Barlow (1994). *Mastering Your Anxiety and Panic—Patient's Workbook.* San Antonio, TX: The Psychological Corporation.

Davis, M., E. Eschelman, and M. McKay (1998). *The Relaxation and Stress Reduction Workbook.* Oakland, CA: New Harbinger.

Smedes, L. (1997). *The Art of Forgiving.* New York: Ballantine.

Child Abuse/Neglect

Hagan, K., and J. Case (1988). *When Your Child Has Been Molested.* Lexington, MA: Lexington Books.

Hindman, J. (1983). *A Very Touchy Book.....For Little People and for Big People.* Durkee, OR: McClure-Hindman Associates.

Jance, J. (1985). *It's Not Your Fault.* Charlotte, NC: Kidsrights.

Katherine, A. (1991). *Boundaries: Where You End and I Begin.* New York: Simon & Schuster.

Crime Victim Trauma

Kliman, A. S. (1978). *Crisis: Psychological First Aid for Recovery and Growth.* Northvale, NJ: Jason Aronson, Inc.

Lerner, H. (1985). *The Dance of Anger*. New York: Harper Row.
Smedes, L. (1997). *The Art of Forgiving*. New York: Ballantine.

Critical Incidents with Emergency Service Providers (ESPs)

Everly, G. S. (1989). *A Clinical Guide to the Treatment of the Human Stress Response*. New York: Plenum.
Mitchell, J. T., and G. Everly (1996). *Critical Incident Stress Debriefing: An Operations Manual for the Prevention of Traumatic Stress Among Emergency Services and Disaster Workers*. Ellicott City, MD: Chevron Publishing.
Peck, M. S. (1993). *Further Along the Road Less Traveled*. New York: Simon & Schuster.
Robinson, B. (1993). *Overdoing It*. Deerfield Beach, FL: Health Communications, Inc.

Depression

Burns, D. (1980). *Feeling Good: The New Mood Therapy*. New York: Signet.
Burns, D. (1989). *The Feeling Good Handbook*. New York: Plume.
Burns, D. (1993). *Ten Days to Self-Esteem!* New York: William Morrow.
Halliman, P. K. (1976). *One Day at a Time*. Minneapolis, MN: CompCare.
Monk, G., et al. (1997). *Narrative Therapy in Practice*. San Francisco: Jossey-Bass.

Disaster

American Red Cross (1991). *Disaster Mental Health Services: Disaster Services Regulations and Procedures*. Alexandria, VA: Author.
Raphael, B. (1986). *When Disaster Strikes*. New York: Basic Books.

Domestic Violence

Ackerman, H. (1985). *The War Against Women: Overcoming Female Abuse*. San Francisco: Harper Hazelden.
Betancourt, M., and R. McAfee (1997). *What to Do When Love Turns Violent: A Practical Resource for Women in Abusive Relationships*. New York: Harper Perrenial Library.
Ens, G., and J. Black (1997). *It's Not Okay Anymore*. Oakland, CA: New Harbinger.
NiCarthy, G. (1984). *Getting Free: You Can End Abuse and Take Back Your Life*. Seattle, WA: The Seal Press.

Paleg, K. (1989). "Spouse Abuse." In M. McKay, P. Rogers, and J. McKay (Eds.), *When Anger Hurts*. Oakland, CA: New Harbinger.

Syzmanski, S. (1985). *Violence Against Women: A Curriculum for Empowerment*. New York: Women's Education Institute.

Walker, L. (1979). *The Battered Woman*. New York: Harper & Row.

Generalized Anxiety Disorder

Beck, A., and G. Emery (1985). *Anxiety Disorders and Phobias: A Cognitive Perspective*. New York: Basic Books.

Bourne, E. (1995). *The Anxiety and Phobia Workbook*. Oakland, CA: New Harbinger Publications.

Burns, D. (1993). *Ten Days to Self-Esteem!* New York: William Morrow.

Leith, L. (1998). *Exercising Your Way to Better Mental Health*. Morgantown, WV: Fitness Information Technology.

Smith, M. (1985). *When I Say No I Feel Guilty*. New York: Bantam Books.

Job Loss

Bolles, R. (1998). *What Color Is Your Parachute?* Berkeley, CA: Ten Speed Press.

Charland, R. (1993). *Career Shifting: Starting Over in a Changing Economy*. Holbrook, MA: Bob Adams.

Loungo, T. (1997). *10 Minute Guide to Household Budgeting*. New York: Macmillan.

Medically Caused Death (Adult)

Bozarth-Campbell, A. (1982). *Life Is Goodbye, Life Is Hello: Grieving Well Through All Kinds of Losses*. Minneapolis, MN: CompCare Press.

Grollman, E. A. (1995). *Living When a Loved One Has Died*. New York: Beacon Press.

Kushner, H. (1981). *When Bad Things Happen to Good People*. New York: Schocken Books.

Rando, T. (1984). *Grief, Dying and Death*. New York: Research Press.

Zonnebelt-Smeenge, S., and R. DeVries (1998). *Getting to the Other Side of Grief: Overcoming the Loss of a Spouse*. Grand Rapids, MI: Baker.

Medically Caused Death (Child)

Dew, R. (1996). *Rachel's Cry—A Journey Through Grief*. Knoxville, TN: Tennessee Valley Publishing.

Finkbeiner, A. (1996). *After the Death of a Child: Living with Loss Through the Years*. New York: Free Press.

Gray, J. (1992). *Men Are From Mars, Women Are From Venus*. New York: Harper-Collins.

Grollman, E. A. (1995). *Living When a Loved One Has Died*. New York: Beacon Press.

Hagan Arnold, J., and P. Buschman-Gemma (1994). *A Child Dies: A Portrait of Family Grief*. Rockville, MD: Aspen System Corporation.

Kushner, H. (1981). *When Bad Things Happen to Good People*. New York: Schocken Books.

Rando, T. (1984). *Grief, Dying and Death*. New York: Research Press.

Schiff, N. (1977). *The Bereaved Parent*. New York: Crown.

Veltman-Grotenhuis, E. (1992). *Song of Triumph*. Grand Rapids, MI: Baker Book House.

Miscarriage/Stillbirth/Abortion

Ilse, S. (1982). *Empty Arms: A Guide to Help Parents and Loved Ones Cope with Miscarriage, Stillbirth and Newborn Death*. Long Lake, MN: Wintergreen Press.

Ilse, S. (1985). *Miscarriage: A Shattered Dream*. Long Lake, MN: Wintergreen Press.

Kubler-Ross, E. (1969). *On Death and Dying*. New York: McMillan Co.

Leith, L. (1998). *Exercising Your Way to Better Mental Health*. Morgantown, WV: Fitness Information Technology.

Schiff, H. (1977). *The Bereaved Parent*. New York: Crown.

Phobias

Beck, A., and G. Emery (1985). *Anxiety Disorders and Phobias: A Cognitive Perspective*. New York: Basic Books.

Bourne, E. (1995). *The Anxiety and Phobia Workbook*. Oakland, CA: New Harbinger Publications.

Brown, J. (1995). *No More Monsters in the Closet*. New York: Prince Paperbacks.

Leith, L. (1998). *Exercising Your Way to Better Mental Health*. Morgantown, WV: Fitness Information Technology.

Wilson, R. (1986). *Don't Panic: Taking Control of Anxiety Attacks*. New York: Harper & Row.

Posttraumatic Stress Disorder (PTSD)

Beck, A., and G. Emery (1985). *Anxiety Disorders and Phobias: A Cognitive Perspective*. New York: Basic Books.

Bourne, E. (1995). *The Anxiety and Phobia Workbook.* Oakland, CA: New Harbinger Publications.

Drews, T. R. (1980). *Getting The Sober: A Guide for Those Living with Alcoholism.* South Plainfield, NJ: Bridge Publishing.

Rosellini, G., and M. Worden (1986). *Of Course You're Angry.* San Francisco: Harper Hazelden.

Rubin, T. I. (1969). *The Angry Book.* New York: Macmillan.

Weisinger, H. (1985). *Dr. Weisinger's Anger Work Out Book.* New York: Quill.

School Trauma: Preelementary

Ginott, H. (1965). *Between Parent and Child.* New York: MacMillan.

Ilf, F., L. Amers, and S. Baker (1981). *Child Behavior: Specific Advice on Problems of Child Behavior.* New York: Harper and Row.

Kerns, L. (1993). *Helping Your Depressed Child.* Rocklin, CA: Prima.

Sanford, D. (1993). *It Won't Last Forever.* Sisters, OR: Quester Publishers.

School Trauma: Elementary

Dobson, J. (1978). *The Strong Willed Child.* Wheaton, IL: Tyndale House.

Fraiberg, S. (1959). *The Magic Years.* New York: Scribners.

Ingersoll, B., and S. Goldstein (1995). *Lonely, Sad and Angry: A Parent's Guide to Depression in Children and Adolescents.* New York: Doubleday.

Millman, H., and C. Schaefer (1977). *Therapies for Children: A Handbook of Effective Treatments for Problem Behaviors.* San Francisco: Jossey-Bass.

School Trauma: Secondary

Black, C. (1982). *It Will Never Happen to Me.* Denver, CO: MAC Printing and Publishing.

Dumont, L. (1991). *Surviving Adolescence: Helping Your Child Through the Struggle.* New York: Villard Books.

Elkind, D. (1984). *All Grown Up and No Place to Go: Teenagers in Crisis.* New York: Addison-Wesley.

McCauey, C. S., and R. Schachter (1988). *When Your Child Is Afraid.* New York: Simon & Schuster.

School Trauma: College

Davis, M., E. Eshelman, and M. McKay (1988). *The Relaxation and Stress Reduction Workbook.* Oakland, CA: New Hampshire.

Helmstetter, S. (1986). *What to Say When You Talk to Yourself.* New York: Fine Communications.

Kasl-Davis, C. (1992). *Many Roads, One Journey.* New York: Harper & Row.

McKay, M., P. Rogers, and J. McKay (1989). *When Anger Hurts.* Oakland CA: New Harbinger.

School Trauma: Staff

Marks, I. (1980). *Living with Fear: Understanding and Coping with Anxiety.* New York: McGraw-Hill.

Matskakis, A. (1992). *I Can't Get Over It: A Handbook for Trauma Survivors.* Oakland, CA: New Harbinger.

Seligman, M. (1990). *Learned Optimism: The Skill To Conquer Life's Obstacles, Large and Small.* New York: Pocket Books.

Simon, S., and S. Simon (1990). *Forgiving: How to Make Peace with Your Past and Get On with Your Life.* New York: Warner Books.

Sexual Assault / Rape

Adams, C., and J. Fay (1989). *Free of the Shadows.* Oakland, CA: New Harbinger.

Gorski, T. (1993). *Getting Love Right: Learning the Choices of Healthy Intimacy.* New York: Simon & Schuster.

Raine, N. (1999). *After Silence: Rape and My Journey Back.* New York: Three Rivers Press.

Roberts, D. (1981). *Raped.* Grand Rapids, MI: Zondervan.

Stalking Victim

Spence-Diehl, E. (1999). *Stalking: A Handbook for Victims.* Holmes Beach, FL: Learning Publications.

Snow, R. *Stopping a Stalker: A Cop's Guide to Making the System Work for You.* Cambridge, MA: Perseus Press.

Wright, C. (1999). *Everything You Need to Know About Dealing With Stalking.* Chicago: Rosen Publishing Group.

Sudden/Accidental Death (Adult)

Colgrove, M. (1976). *How to Survive the Loss of a Loved One.* New York: Bloomfield & McWilliams.

Kushner, H. (1981). *When Bad Things Happen to Good People.* New York: Schocken Books.

Smedes, L. (1982). *How Can It Be All Right When Everything Is All Wrong?* San Francisco: Harper.

Zonnebelt-Smeenge, S., and R. DeVries (1998). *Getting to the Other Side of Grief: Overcoming the Loss of a Spouse*. Grand Rapids, MI: Baker Book House.

Sudden/Accidental Death (Child)

Hagan Arnold, J., and P. Buschman-Gemma (1994). *A Child Dies: A Portrait of Family Grief*. Rockville, MD: Aspen System Corporation.
Kushner, H. (1981). *When Bad Things Happen to Good People*. New York: Schocken Books.
Schiff, H. (1977). *The Bereaved Parent*. New York: Crown.
Westberg, G. (1962). *Good Grief*. Philadelphia: Fortress Press.

Suicide (Adult)

Fine, C. (1997). *No Time to Say Goodbye*. New York: Doubleday.
Jamison, K. R. (1999). *Night Falls Fast: Understanding Suicide*. New York: Knopf.
Rando, T. (1984). *Grief, Dying and Death*. New York: Research Press.
Smolin, A. (1993). *Healing After the Suicide of a Loved One*. New York: Fireside.

Suicide (Child)

Dumont, L. (1991). *Surviving Adolescence: Helping Your Child Through the Struggle*. New York: Villard Books.
Fine, C. (1997). *No Time to Say Goodbye*. New York: Doubleday.
Hagan Arnold, J., and P. Buschman-Gemma (1994). *A Child Dies: A Portrait of Family Grief*. Rockville, MD: Aspen System Corporation.
McCoy, K. (1994). *Understanding Your Teenager's Depression*. New York: Perigee.
Wholey, D. (1992). *When the Worst That Can Happen Already Has*. New York: Hyperion.

Workplace Violence

Cal-OSHA (1994). *Guidelines for Workplace Security*. San Francisco, CA: Department of Industrial Relations.
Flannery, R. B. (1998). *The Assaulted Staff Action Program*. Ellicott City, MD: Chevron.
O'Hara, V. (1995). *Five Weeks to Healing Stress*. Oakland, CA: New Harbinger.

Appendix B

INDEX OF DSM-IV™ CODES ASSOCIATED WITH PRESENTING PROBLEMS

Academic Problem   **V62.3**
School Trauma: Preelementary
School Trauma: Elementary
School Trauma: Secondary
School Trauma: College

Acute Stress Disorder   **308.3**
Acute Stress Disorder
Child Abuse/Neglect
Crime Victim Trauma
Critical Incidents with Emergency
   Service Providers (ESPs)
Disasters
Domestic Violence
Generalized Anxiety Disorder
Job Loss
Medically Caused Death (Adult)
Medically Caused Death (Child)
Miscarriage/Stillbirth/Abortion
Posttraumatic Stress Disorder (PTSD)
School Trauma (Preelementary)
School Trauma (Elementary)
School Trauma (Secondary)
School Trauma (College)
School Trauma (Staff)
Sexual Assault/Rape
Stalking Victim
Sudden/Accidental Death (Adult)
Sudden/Accidental Death (Child)

Suicide (Adult)
Suicide (Child)
Workplace Violence

Adjustment Disorder   **309.xx**
Child Abuse/Neglect
Crime Victim Trauma
Critical Incidents with Emergency
   Service Providers (ESPs)
Disasters
Job Loss
Medically Caused Death (Adult)
Medically Caused Death (Child)
Posttraumatic Stress Disorder (PTSD)
School Trauma (Preelementary)
School Trauma (Elementary)
School Trauma (Secondary)
School Trauma (College)
School Trauma (Staff)
Sudden/Accidental Death (Adult)
Sudden/Accidental Death (Child)
Suicide (Adult)
Suicide (Child)

**Adjustment Disorder
with Anxiety**   **309.24**
Acute Stress Disorder
Domestic Violence
Generalized Anxiety Disorder

Sudden/Accidental Death (Adult)
Sudden/Accidental Death (Child)

Depersonalization Disorder   300.6
Posttraumatic Stress Disorder (PTSD)
Sexual Assault/Rape
Workplace Violence

Diagnosis Deferred   799.9
School Trauma (College)

Dissociative Amnesia   300.12
Posttraumatic Stress Disorder (PTSD)
Sexual Assault/Rape
Workplace Violence

**Dissociative Identity
Disorder   300.14**
Posttraumatic Stress Disorder (PTSD)
School Trauma (Preelementary)
Workplace Violence

Dysthymic Disorder   300.4
Crime Victim Trauma
Critical Incidents with Emergency
   Service Providers (ESPs)
Depression
Domestic Violence
Posttraumatic Stress Disorder (PTSD)
School Trauma (Staff)
Sexual Assault/Rape
Stalking Victim
Suicide (Adult)
Suicide (Child)

Encopresis   307.7
School Trauma (Preelementary)
School Trauma (Elementary)

Enuresis   307.6
School Trauma (Preelementary)
School Trauma (Elementary)

Generalized Anxiety Disorder 300.02
Acute Stress Disorder
Crime Victim Trauma
Disasters
Generalized Anxiety Disorder
Phobias
Posttraumatic Stress Disorder (PTSD)
School Trauma (Secondary)
School Trauma (College)
School Trauma (Staff)

**Histrionic Personality
Disorder   301.50**
Acute Stress Disorder
Crime Victim Trauma
Depression
Disasters
Domestic Violence
Generalized Anxiety Disorder
Phobias
Posttraumatic Stress Disorder (PTSD)
School Trauma (Staff)
Sexual Assault/Rape

Major Depressive Disorder   296.xx
Crime Victim Trauma
Disasters
Domestic Violence
Posttraumatic Stress Disorder (PTSD)
School Trauma (Staff)
Sexual Assault/Rape
Stalking Victim
Suicide (Adult)
Suicide (Child)

**Major Depressive Disorder,
Recurrent   296.3x**
Depression

**Major Depressive Disorder,
Single Episode   296.2x**
Critical Incidents with Emergency
   Service Providers (ESPs)
Depression
Job Loss
Medically Caused Death (Adult)
Medically Caused Death (Child)
Miscarriage/Stillbirth/Abortion
School Trauma (Secondary)
School Trauma (College)
Sudden/Accidental Death (Adult)
Sudden/Accidental Death (Child)
Workplace Violence

Malingering   V65.2
Critical Incidents with Emergency
   Service Providers (ESPs)
Job Loss
Posttraumatic Stress Disorder (PTSD)
Stalking Victim

Neglect of Child (Victim)   995.5
Child Abuse/Neglect

ABOUT THE DISK*

TheraScribe® 3.0 and 3.5 Library Module Installation

The enclosed disk contains files to upgrade your TheraScribe® 3.0 or 3.5 program to include the behavioral definitions, goals, objectives, and interventions from *The Traumatic Events Treatment Planner.*

Note: You must have TheraScribe® 3.0 or 3.5 for Windows installed on your computer in order to use *The Traumatic Events Treatment Planner* library module.

To install the library module, please follow these steps:

1. Place the library module disk in your floppy drive.
2. Log in to TheraScribe® 3.0 or 3.5 as the Administrator using the name "Admin" and your administrator password.
3. On the Main Menu, press the "GoTo" button, and choose the Options menu item.
4. Press the "Import Library" button.
5. On the Import Library Module screen, choose your floppy disk drive a:\ from the list and press "Go." Note: It may take a few minutes to import the data from the floppy disk to your computer's hard disk.
6. When the installation is complete, the library module data will be available in your TheraScribe® 3.0 or 3.5 program.

Note: If you have a network version of TheraScribe® 3.0 or 3.5 installed, you should import the library module one time only. After importing the data, the library module data will be available to all network users.

User Assistance

If you need assistance using this TheraScribe® 3.0 or 3.5 add-on module, contact Wiley Technical Support at:

Phone: 212-850-6753
Fax: 212-850-6800 (Attention: Wiley Technical Support)
E-mail: techhelp@wiley.com

---

*Note: This section applies only to the book with disk edition, ISBN 0-471-39588-9.

For information on how to install disk, refer to the **About the Disk** section on page 257.